MISSION SYMPHONY
Notes for the Third Millennium

with Leader's Guide

To George & Marianna long-time friends and fellow gourmands (not to forget "Presbyterians") — this is our song!! — Thanks for your friendship and hospitality (and coming to Deep Run today.)

WILLIAM E. CHAPMAN

W. E. Chapman

April 6, 2006

Witherspoon Press
Louisville, Kentucky

Publisher: *Sandra Moak Sorem*
Editor: *Martha Gilliss*
Cover design and book interior: *Carol E. Johnson*

First edition
Published by Witherspoon Press
Louisville, Kentucky

Web site address: www.pcusa.org/witherspoon

PRINTED IN THE UNITED STATES OF AMERICA
04 05 06 07 08 09 10 11 12 13—10 9 8 7 6 5 4 3 2 1

Library of Congress Cataloging-in-Publication Data

Chapman, William E.
  Mission symphony / William E. Chapman.— 1st ed.
    p. cm.
  "With a leader's guide".
  Includes bibliographical references and index.
  ISBN 1-57153-049-5
  1. Presbyterian Church (U.S.A.) Church and its mission. 2. Presbyterian Church (U.S.A.)—Doctrines. 3. Mission of the church. I. Title.
  BX8969.6.P743C485 2004
  266'.5137—dc22
                                    2004008288

CONTENTS

—

Program Note . . . . *v*

Overture 1

The Church and Its Mission (*Book of Order,* G-3.0000) 5

First Movement: God 10

    Maestoso (G-3.0101a) 10

    Lamentoso (G-3.0101b) 17

    Processional (G-3.0102) 20

    Mazurka (G-3.0103) 25

Second Movement: Church 30

    Fugue (G-3.0200) 30

Third Movement: Called 43

    Chorale (G-3.0300) 43

Fourth Movement: Challenged 60

    Sprung Time (G-3.0400) 60

    Postlude 75

A Final Reflection 78

Leader's Guide 80

Additional Resources 89

PROGRAM NOTE

—

Thank you for coming to the threshold for a symphony. As you settle into your chair, I hope you are prepared to ponder what you will encounter. You may already have noticed the musical language in this book. The musical metaphor of this book arose when I let the text of G-3.000 speak to me. I hope it also speaks to you in ways beyond what you will find in these pages.

You will find that *Mission Symphony* is, like Franz Schubert's "Unfinished Symphony," unfinished in several ways. Mission is what Christians do. Mission is how we respond to God's call in Christ, a call that persists throughout time. Each of us as a believer is thus a player in this grand symphony. The audience for our symphony is, as Kierkegaard suggested, an audience of one: God. The same God is also the conductor, always working with us to improve our performance.

The musical metaphor offers an alternative to the religious discussions and debates we American Presbyterians have had for our two centuries on this North American continent. I suggest that it is time to move into a new mode of going about mission, one where what we produce together, as players in a grand orchestra and choir, is how we consider our faithfulness to Jesus Christ.

This project was just beginning as the 214th General Assembly (2003) met in Denver, Colorado. The "prelude" for the opening worship, written by John Kuzma, minister of music of the Montview Presbyterian Church, demonstrated how the rich diversity of our denomination could be expressed musically in a symphony of praise. Different styles of music, an amazing array of instruments, and varying moods came together through Kuzma's genius to demonstrate in a deeply moving and beautiful way what we as Presbyterians are at our best. I hope that perhaps someone will find in these pages the inspiration for a truly musical version of *Mission Symphony*.

Music affects all of us, yet differently. When music moves me, I consider that good music. Different musical qualities move us in different ways. My hope is that G-3.0000, this sketch of the mission symphony written in the late 1970s and early 1980s and adopted in 1983, will move others as it has moved me to give greater glory to God, and to find increased vigor for our mission together as Presbyterians. If you want to contact me, I will be happy to hear from you by e-mail to polywonk@aol.com.

I am deeply grateful for several colleagues who assisted me during this enterprise. My first appreciation is to Hila G. Chapman, who nurtured in me love and deep appreciation for music and musicians. Stated Clerk Clifton Kirkpatrick has alerted us to the generally unappreciated significance of the first four chapters of the *Book of Order* and proposed that I explore something of this theme through the lens of the musical metaphor. Fellow scribbler Clifford Sherrod has waded through each of my books with his poet's eye, testing whether there was any sense to what I had composed. Rev. Dwight A. White, our General Assembly Council colleague who shares a lifelong passion for mission, was another reader for this book. Fran Thiessen honed my attempts to use musical terms, thereby making me appear more knowledgeable in that area than I am. The folks at Witherspoon Press continue to provide outstanding editorial services. My deepest thanks go to my wife, Zitta, who does the original correcting of my English, but more important provides the continuing loving support that makes such a project possible. Without these, and a host of teachers and colleagues whose contributions are woven into these pages, there would not have been this music.

OVERTURE

—◆—

Chapter III of the Presbyterian Church (U.S.A.)'s *Book of Order*, Part One, Form of Government, begins with a twenty-three-word definition of mission for Presbyterians (see below).

I propose that we consider this definition, from a musical perspective, as an overture. For instance, Beethoven begins his Fifth Symphony with an initial statement of a four-note theme on which he will build the rest of the work. On first hearing those notes, one wonders how such a simple sequence of sounds can become a symphony. Yet as one listens with those notes in mind, Beethoven's mastery of his craft emerges.

It is helpful to think of the first sentence of G-3.0100 as the opening strains of a symphony. When presented in boldface type, the key words of the chapter become evident:

> The **mission** of the **Church** is given form by **God**'s activity in the **world** as told in the Bible and understood by **faith**.

"The Mission of the Church" is the topic to be defined, the title of the symphony. The other four words serve as the framework of movements for the symphony, the motifs that will be explored so that their richness and power can be appreciated.

The foundation for the "mission of the Church" is God. *God* is mentioned 25 times in this definition. Considering that the boldface key words appear a total of 73 times in chapter III, God is very important for a Presbyterian understanding of mission. It is also significant that *Jesus* is used 8 times and *Christ* 13 times, which increases the total to 46 times, almost two-thirds of the occurrence of the key words.

1

As the themes are developed, the qualification in the initial statement, that God's activity is the focus, becomes more evident. In contrast to G-1.0100, where God's intent regarding the re-creation of God's people through the life and work of Jesus Christ as Savior and Lord is discussed theologically, this chapter focuses on God's activity.[1] It is what God has done and is doing that provides direction for the Church.

The second key word in this definition is *Church*. The capital letter **C** stands for a wider community than those people with whom we worship and work, though it includes us and them. Presbyterians recognize that our profession of faith in Jesus Christ makes us a part of the larger Church, including those we meet in governing bodies beyond the session. The long Presbyterian tradition of ecumenical involvement spreads the circle of faith even wider.[2] The word *Church* appears 10 times in this chapter.

Consistent with the Confession of 1967, this initial announcement of the key motifs indicates that mission is the business of the Church. "God's reconciling work in Jesus Christ and the mission of reconciliation to which he has called his church are at the heart of the gospel in any age."[3] We will have opportunity to explore the connection between the Confession of 1967 and G-3.0000. For now, it is sufficient to recognize how these two documents provide substance to the theme of chapter III.

The third key word is *world*. "That God so loved the world" introduces John 3:16, a fragment of Scripture that most Protestants know. *World* appears 10 times in G-3.0000. This motif is developed in interesting and unexpected ways, ways that are refreshing and challenging to customary understandings as this chapter proceeds.

Faith is present throughout this chapter, implicitly rather than explicitly (except for the first sentence). The word *faith* appears three times in this chapter.[4] It will become evident that faith is a leitmotif, a subtle theme developing through the course of the chapter.

Each paragraph will be presented as a separate movement in this symphony, ending with a return to the initial statement. Along the way, the musical metaphor will develop as the different movements emerge. There will be changes in mood and tempo as the symphony develops. The conclusion comes as a turn from appreciation to participation, to responding to God's call.

"Movement" is a key concept that serves to keep the key words together, as it suggests overtones of dynamism, action, intention.

These are essential for any discussion of our mission as Presbyterians. While most of us agree that mission is essential to the Christian life, the issue that troubles us is knowing what sort of action is required. For some, mission requires geographical and international movement, carrying the good news of Christ to the ends of the earth. To others, mission is moving out into any area of suffering and human need, wherever it is on the planet, even in our own backyards.

I learned this theme at home, growing up. Both emphases were present whenever my family sat down to a meal. I learned early on that debates about mission were family quarrels, matters that could move discussions into arguments, and even beyond, because my father had a fundamental orientation, while my mother's views were more modern. What I learned at home has been true of our Presbyterian family for centuries. It is a fact of life for us. Distressingly, we seem unable to agree that mission is multifaceted, a responsibility that goes beyond what any of us are able to do.

Chapter III of the Form of Government in our *Book of Order* reminds us that our mission always needs to be faithful to God's activity in the world. God, who endows the Church with a diversity of gifts, calls each of us to respond in faith and love in community with others. God works in many ways through God's Spirit. Humility requires us to celebrate God's activity, however it is accomplished and by whomever. To decide that the Christian mission can be accomplished in only one way is to intrude on God's sovereignty. Such a stark way of settling the point may remind all of us that we must, for the sake of the gospel, work together.

As we discuss what chapter III has to say about mission, let us bear in mind that it is God's action we are called to assist. When we read that mission is "given form by God's activity in the world," let us carry with us the understanding that mission is not only work on behalf of the church; it must also be implemented as God in Christ has shown us in Scripture and faith. We will never achieve a perfect duplication of "God's activity in the world," but we can remind one another that we are all, with our different and even diverse gifts, seeking together to be faithful witnesses.

NOTES

1. For reflections on G-1.0100, see William E. Chapman, *Finding Christ . . . in the Book of Order* (Louisville: Witherspoon Press, 2003).
2. Note G-2.0300–.0400, where the broader community of faith is articulated. Also pertinent are G-15.0000, "Relationships"; 16.0000; "Union Churches"; Appendix C, "A Formula of Agreement"; Appendix D, "A Statement of Ecumenical Consensus."
3. *Book of Confessions,* 9.06.
4. *Faith* is referred to extensively in G-2.0000, "The Church and Its Confessions."

THE CHURCH AND
ITS MISSION[1]

—

First Movement

G-3.0100 Form

The mission of the Church is given form
by God's activity in the world
as told in the Bible
and understood by faith.

G-3.0101a God's Activity

God created the heavens and the earth and
made human beings in God's image,
charging them to care for all that lives;
God made men and women
    to live in community,
    responding to their Creator
        with grateful obedience.
Even when the human race broke community with its Maker
and with one another,
    God did not forsake it,
        but out of grace
            chose one family for the sake of all,
            to be pilgrims of promise,
            God's own Israel.

---

1. From the *Book of Order*, Form of Government, chapter III.

G-3.0101b God's Covenant

God liberated the people of Israel from oppression;
God covenanted with Israel to be their God and
    they to be God's people,
        that they might do justice, love mercy, and walk humbly
        with the Lord;
God confronted Israel with the responsibilities of this covenant,
    judging the people for their unfaithfulness
    while sustaining them by divine grace.

G-3.0102 God in Christ

God was incarnate in Jesus Christ,
    who announced good news to the poor,
    proclaimed release for prisoners and
    recovery of sight for the blind,
    let the broken victims go free, and
    proclaimed the year of the Lord's favor.
Jesus came to seek and to save the lost;
      in his life and death for others
      God's redeeming love for all people was made visible;
    and in the resurrection of Jesus Christ
      there is the assurance of God's victory over sin and
        death and
      the promise of God's continuing presence in the world.

G-3.0103 The Holy Spirit

God's redeeming and reconciling activity in the world
    continues through the presence and power of the Holy Spirit,
    who confronts individuals and societies
      with Christ's Lordship of life and
      calls them to repentance and
      to obedience to the will of God.

Second Movement

G-3.0200 The Church as the Body of Christ

The Church of Jesus Christ is
the provisional demonstration
    of what God intends for all of humanity.

G-3.0200a

    The Church is called to be a sign
        in and for the world
        of the new reality
            which God has made available to people in Jesus Christ.

G-3.0200b

    The new reality revealed in Jesus Christ is
        the new humanity,
        a new creation,
        a new beginning for human life in the world:
            Sin is forgiven.
            Reconciliation is accomplished.
            The dividing walls of hostility are torn down.

G-3.0200c

    The Church is the body of Christ,
        both in its corporate life and
        in the lives of its individual members,
        and is called to give shape and substance to this truth.

Third Movement

G-3.0300a The Church's Calling

    The Church is called
        to tell the good news of salvation
            by the grace of God
            through faith in Jesus Christ as the only Savior and Lord,
    proclaiming in Word and Sacrament that
        the new age has dawned.
        God who creates life,
            frees those in bondage,
            forgives sin,
            reconciles brokenness,
            makes all things new,
            is still at work in the world.

G-3.0300b Present Claims of Christ

The Church is called
   to present the claims of Jesus Christ,
      leading persons to repentance,
      acceptance of him as Savior and Lord, and
      new life as his disciples.

G-3.0300c Christ's Faithful Evangelist

The Church is called
   to be Christ's faithful evangelist
      going into the world,
      making disciples of all nations,
      baptizing them in the name of the Father and of the Son
         and of the Holy Spirit,
      teaching them to observe all he has commanded;
   demonstrating by the love of its members
      for one another and
      by the quality of its common life
         the new reality in Christ;
         sharing in worship, fellowship, and nurture,
         practicing a deepened life of prayer and service
            under the guidance of the Holy Spirit;
   participating in God's activity in the world through its life
      for others by
      a. healing and reconciling and binding up wounds,
      b. ministering to the needs of the poor, the sick, the
         lonely, and the powerless,
      c. engaging in the struggle to free people from sin,
         fear, oppression, hunger, and injustice,
      d. giving itself and its substance to the service of those
         who suffer,
      e. sharing with Christ in the establishing of his
         just, peaceable, and loving rule in the world.

Fourth Movement

G-3.0400 Called to Risk and Trust

The Church is called to undertake this mission
    even at the risk of losing its life,
        trusting in God alone as the author and giver of life,
        sharing the gospel, and
        doing those deeds in the world that
            point beyond themselves to the new reality in Christ.

G-3.0401 Called to Openness

The Church is called:

a. to a new openness to the presence of God in the Church and
      in the world,
    to more fundamental obedience, and
    to a more joyous celebration in worship and work;

b. to a new openness to its own membership,
      by affirming itself as a community of diversity,
      becoming in fact as well as in faith a community of
      women and men of all ages, races, and conditions, and
      by providing for inclusiveness as a visible sign of the
        new humanity;

c. to a new openness to the possibilities and perils
      of its institutional forms
      in order to ensure the faithfulness and usefulness
      of these forms to God's activity in the world;

d. to a new openness to God's continuing reformation of the
    Church ecumenical,
      that it might be a more effective instrument of mission
        in the world.

1
FIRST MOVEMENT: GOD

Maestoso (G-3.0101a)

The mission symphony opens with God at work, creating. There-
fore, any Presbyterian discussion of mission must begin theologically. Deep roots in faith deter a mission enterprise from veering
away from faithful proclamation of the good news. At the same
time, commitment to mission insulates theology from sterility.
Theology and mission belong together, need one another.

What is titled "The Church and Its Mission"[1] begins with Genesis 1. There are two objects of the verb *created:* heaven and earth.
That God created "the heavens and the earth" is so basic that further comment is omitted. Nor is the "how" necessary. It is the fact
that matters, however, the scope of mission is already established:
the cosmos. Already the theme of *world* has appeared as the stage
for mission.

Paired with *created* is the verb *made,* which introduces the focus
of God's creation: human beings. The link between these creatures
and the Creator is "God's image." Eugene Peterson expands the
meaning of "God's image" in his paraphrase of Ephesians 1:4:
"Long before [God] laid down earth's foundations he had us in
mind."[2] Just what the phrase "image of God" means is the subject
of much scholarly discussion.[3]

Our *Book of Confessions,* Part I of The Constitution of the Presbyterian Church (U.S.A.), offers ten citations relating to the
"image of God."[4] Most of these are assertions that humankind is
made in God's image. The Heidelberg Catechism uses the phrase

as a way of explaining why obeying the Ten Commandments is important.[5] The Larger Catechism defines the image in the final phrase by indicating the attributes of "knowledge, righteousness and holiness, having the law of God written in their hearts, and power to fulfill it, with dominion over the creatures."[6] A Brief Statement of Faith has four lines expressing a perspective on this phrase:

> In sovereign love God created the world good
>   and makes everyone equally in God's image,
>   male and female, of every race and people,
>   to live as one community.[7]

However we may think of the "image of God," the way human creation emerges in this first movement of the Mission Symphony highlights the fact that God's creation is an act of love.

There is one more phrase in this first clause, a significant addition for constructing a basis for mission: "charging [human beings] to care for all that lives." All humanity is brought into being by an act of divine love—not just you and me as Presbyterians. To assert that human beings are created in God's image is to require reverence for one another.

We all, every human, begin on this level playing field. The trappings of culture and success, of status and social position, of any mark that allegedly differentiates between people, all these things dissolve in the bright light of God's creation. Whatever apparent distinguishing marks suggest privilege and power never diminish our responsibility to care for one another. A hallmark of mission for any believer is that we are all in this world together, trying to figure out how we can live together as those who are in some way very much like the Creator.

Already a valid understanding of mission accepts the priority of caring for "all that lives." The remainder of this sentence after the semicolon develops two elements of what sort of caring is appropriate in mission. The first is, "God made men and women to live in community." As Everett Fox puts it in his contemporary Jewish paraphrase of the Scripture passage echoing (Gen. 2:18) in this phrase:

> Now YHWH, God, said:
> It is not good for the human to be alone,
> I will make him a helper corresponding to him.

In a footnote Fox offers us another translation of "a helper: a helping counterpart."[8] Humans were created to live in community. We are social beings at our core. There is an inherent desire for mutuality that comes from deep within us.

But there is more to us than our mutuality. Responding to one another as humans is not the whole story. The community we seek as humans has another dimension. This sentence ends with a qualification: ". . . responding to their Creator with grateful obedience." In Genesis 2, Eve responds to the serpent with her understanding of their role, to eat the fruit of the garden, but not of the tree in the center. The tempting serpent suggests that there won't be any consequences if they do what they want, a suggestion that produces dire results.

Fox indicates that the Ten Commandments are distinctive for the time and place, in that God "sets forth demands, with no punishments listed."[9] His comment is consistent with the Garden of Eden incident. Fox expresses the commandments in the form "You are not to . . . ," which softens the traditional, "Thou shalt not . . . " of the King James version. Commandments are God's directions regarding what a life of gratitude looks like.

The absence of expressed punishments for noncompliance suggests to us a paradox. While a simple imperative seems to open up the range of choices one may make, there is also our uneasiness about making "the wrong choice." We ask, "What happens if I disobey?" I vividly recall my mother telling me to be careful not to put my fingers in a light socket. The consequence of disobedience in that instance was a jolt. Mother still loved me afterward, comforting me even if I had disobeyed her.

Minor Shift

"Even" at the start of the next sentence signals a minor chord intruding into the stately major section. "In spite of" is what "even" conveys. The complication presents a challenge to be resolved. But what is the complication? It is the sort of challenge which Johann Sebastian Bach would cherish, relishing the opportunity to work toward resolution of complex dissonance. A contemporary composer could shift to 7/8 time, introducing an element of uncertainty into what had been majestic and orderly.

"Even when" moves us from creation amid eternity into time and the biblical account of our planet, specifically into Genesis 3.

Instead of using "sin" as is often the case, the disruption is named "the breaking of community." The community God gives human-kind can be broken. Community is durable, yet also vulnerable. Community is a gift that has been, and continues to be, rejected. We cannot be human by ourselves.

However we understand the temptation narrative in Genesis 3, the passage resonates with our experience. We are reminded that the human tendency to test limits, to see what will happen, is not inborn, yet somehow always seems present within us. We look around us in our own church and find those who prefer to stand apart from us on one issue or another, rather than to stand together with us as kinfolk in Christ. We know too well, too intimately, how we ourselves prefer, like Greta Garbo, to be alone.

Separating oneself from one's fellow humans is more than anti-social behavior, as far as we Christians are concerned. It is "break-ing community with [our] Maker" that is the greater problem. The One who gave us community becomes the first victim when we choose to "do it ourselves." Rejecting the gift pushes the Giver away from us. We become isolated, preferring solitude for commu-nity, trying to become something for which we were not created. Harmony becomes irrelevant to melody.

Fortunately, neither the sentence nor the story ends there. The comma hints that although the rebellion seems to have failed, humanity's attempt to "go it alone" is not the last word. The One who gives the gift of community intends that humanity live in community with the Giver as well as with fellow humans.

God "did not forsake" humanity, although that would have been understandable from a human point of view. At this point, God reveals another aspect of God's nature: God "chose a family." The rebellion against community is resolved by creating a family. Com-munity has been re-created, underlining this basic aspect of human-ity, as well as indicating that God's purposes cannot ultimately be thwarted.

As the sentence marches on, the adverbial clause "out of grace" reminds us how this was done, consistent with God's nature. The three words characterize how God makes the choice. Ogden Nash's cryptic couplet

> How odd of God
> To choose the Jews

captures the mystery, the strangeness of God's action. Although the "rediscovery of God's grace"[10] is an appropriate way to describe the Protestant Reformation, William Placher contends that there has been an ongoing struggle by Christians to appreciate the power of grace.[11] The definition of grace as "unmerited favor" seems at first glance insufficient as a way of describing God's amazing love. Yet this two-word phrase suggests how surprising God's grace is, how out of the ordinary.

Unmerited means that one cannot earn it. Grace comes always and only as a gift. We who seek to be faithful are admittedly undeserving. We all rebel against others as our "right," proving only that we deceive ourselves. "There but for the grace of God go I" used to be broadly accepted among church folk. Some I know habitually respond when asked, "How are you doing?" with "Better than I deserve." This response among Christians reminds us that we live by grace, and only by grace.

Grace also suggests a mystery. We finally don't know what it was that led God to choose a family, much less why God chose a particular family. Presbyterians are often thought of as emphasizing predestination. Within the Presbyterian family we have struggled with this heritage. Many understandings swirl through our fellowship. Seldom do we grasp Calvin's point that

> a proper understanding of predestination "builds up faith soundly, trains us to humility, elevates us to admiration of the immense goodness of God towards us, and excites us to praise this goodness."[12]

Eugene Peterson provides an instance of "a proper understanding of predestination" in his paraphrase of Ephesians 1:3–4:

> How blessed is God! And what a blessing he is! He is the Father of our Master, Jesus Christ, and takes us to the high places of blessing in him. Long before he laid down earth's foundations, he had us in mind, had settled on us as the focus of his love, to be made whole and holy by his love.[13]

We live in a time when the word *family* is understood in many different ways. "Alternate family" is a way of describing this modern diversity. We also see strenuous advocacy for various formulations regarding what "family" means. Marilynne Robinson comments,

> I am sure it is no accident that the qualities of patience and respect and loyalty and generosity which would make family

sustainable are held in very low regard among us, some of them even doubling as neuroses such as dependency and lack of assertiveness.[14]

Robinson proposes an imaginary alternative:

> Imagine this: some morning we awake to the cultural consensus that a family, however else defined, is a sort of compact of mutual loyalty, organized around the hope of giving rich, human meaning to the lives of its members. Toward this end they do what people do—play with their babies, comfort their sick, keep their holidays, commemorate their occasions, sing songs, tell jokes, fight and reconcile, teach and learn what they know about what is right and wrong, about what is beautiful and what is to be valued. . . . They are kind and receive kindness, they are generous and are sustained and enriched by others' generosity. The antidote to fear, distrust, self-interest is always loyalty. The balm for failure or weakness, or even disloyalty, is always loyalty.[15]

This is a vision of the sort of family God was seeking as God sought to overcome the disloyalty that tried to break community.[16]

God's reconstituted family is "for the sake of all. . . . " It is not the identity as family, but the "for the sake of" that characterizes God's gracious formation of a group. "All" echoes God's covenant message to Noah after the Flood: "This is the sign of the covenant that I have established between me and all flesh that is on the earth."[17] This is the root for what the *Book of Order* calls "a great theme of the Reformation," "the election of the people of God for service as well as salvation."[18]

G-3.0101a ends with two names for this "one family" God chooses. First, God chooses humans to be "pilgrims of promise." In high school I had a teacher who required us to learn the first twenty lines of Chaucer's *Canterbury Tales* in Middle English. Every day we listened to a record of someone reading the two or so lines we would do that day. Before long, we were able to recite the passage. Fifty years later, the lines are still on my tongue. It was in reading that ancient text that I began to understand what pilgrims were: ordinary folk with mixed aims and motives, moving together in search of some fresher, deeper understanding of themselves, their fellow pilgrims, and their God.

Presbyterians are unlikely pilgrims, in the traditional sense of going to some shrine or holy place. We are not likely to use "pilgrim" language. Many Americans understand the term to refer only to those early immigrants who came to the New World to find religious freedom or to escape from persecution for their dissenting religious beliefs.

Yet we are "pilgrims of promise," a party of hope in a troubled and dangerous world. As I write, our country is on the brink of a "hot war," where troops are mobilized and sent into battle, many of whom will return in body bags, rather than to hugs and handshakes. Maintaining the perspective of those seeking the kingdom of God is a challenge today. It always has been. It is when we forget the promise, and the One whose promise inspires and energizes us, that we lose our direction, that our mission is no longer focused on God's will for all humanity. We are called to be "pilgrims of promise," a title we can bear humbly together.

The other designation, "God's own Israel," seems to intrude, continuing to underscore the same corporate emphasis suggested in "family," while adding another dimension for our consideration. We are catapulted into Genesis 32:13–32, where Jacob wrestles all night with a mysterious assailant and earns a new name, Israel. Up to that time, Jacob is portrayed as a conniver, always scheming to get the advantage over whomever he can. Canadian professor Stanley Walters, commenting on this passage, writes:

> The story, therefore, in an overt polyvalence, blends Jacob's conflict with people and with God into one event. . . . The story is thus made psychologically and theologically profound by superimposing on one another Jacob's need to face his own character, his relations with people, and his relation with God.[19]

Walters goes on to describe how Jacob, who has become Israel at Peniel gives his new name to God's people. Today we associate the word *Israel* with the name of a country in the Middle East recognized in 1948. The biblical roots offer us a "polyvalent" understanding. We see how a dramatic experience of God's gracious and sovereign choice—of a person otherwise considered a scoundrel—becomes the basis for a name and a nation that testify to God's gracious and reconciling love.

Sometimes the Christian fellowship is called "the new Israel." J. Christiaan Beker points out that while this idea is often attributed to the apostle Paul, it was not until A.D. 150 that Barnabas and Justin Martyr directly connected the two terms.[20] Beker notes what

Paul carefully suggested in Romans: "In short, for Paul, the gospel means the extension of the promise beyond Israel to the Gentiles, not the displacement of Israel by the Gentile Church."[21] Such an extension suggests that to consider the Church of Jesus Christ as the "new Israel" is to apply an ambivalent designation, reminding us both of our Jewish cousin community and of our continuing struggles of faith, our wrestling through the challenges that emerge as we seek to fulfill our calling as disciples of Jesus Christ.

"God's activity in the world" is the major emphasis in the first movement of the mission symphony. The text has moved from creation of the world and of humanity through broken community to the beginning of God's calling together a people. We have moved through the first thirty-two chapters of Genesis in a seven-line paragraph. We learn that the God of the Bible is a gracious Creator who desires that humankind live in community, and who goes to great lengths to ensure that the community will persist. We also recognize that there is still the rest of the Old Testament witness to God's activity. The symphony has just begun.

Lamentoso (G-3.0101b)

The second passage in G-3.0101 continues the first movement, now with increased complexity. The text moves from God's promise in the early covenants of Genesis to the complication of the rest of the Old Testament. The musical setting of this section could draw from the major themes of country music, especially bluegrass, where human problems of lost love, misfortune, and laments lie at the roots of expression.

The paragraph picks up the history of Israel, God's chosen people, who have journeyed to Egypt only to be enslaved. The first eight words summarize the first nineteen chapters of Exodus: "God liberated the people of Israel from oppression." Using the verb *liberated* to describe God's activity underscores that God acts in history both for the sake of the chosen community and to demonstrate God's sovereign mercy.

Liberation was a word chosen by Latin American theologians to describe a movement in the late twentieth century proclaiming that the gospel spoke directly to those who suffered inordinately in political and social systems that severely limited opportunities for free expression. This movement frightened many in the United

States for whom "liberation" was a code word for anti-American ideology. The proposal that God was engaged in liberation seemed more than some church folk could accept.

"Liberation" carries a strong political connotation for many Americans. Our Revolutionary War was fought for the sake of liberation of the American colonies from what many considered oppression by the English king. Perhaps it is the apparent combination of civil politics with theological assertion, the appearance of mixing church and state, that triggers the problem. Perhaps what troubles some people is a fear that God's liberation intrudes on our personal struggles for identity and independent responsibility.

An African American spiritual reminds us that the message of Exodus is more than just a "back then" reality for someone else:

> When Israel was in Egypt's land,
> Let my people go!
> Oppressed so hard they could not stand,
> Let my people go![22]

This hymn reminds us that those who have known oppression first-hand, as a physical and mental reality, also recognize that freedom comes only from liberation, that the price is high, and that it is often beyond what human ingenuity and striving can attain.

Oppression refers to things outside us that restrict our ability to go about living normal lives, those forces and conditions that we cannot change by ourselves. The psalmist was oppressed when writing, "Out of the depths I have cried to you, O Lord" (Ps. 130:1).[23] The depths of human experience are manifold, yet their effect on us is consistently negative, generating a sense of inability to escape. Such human dread is addressed by the God who liberates those who cry out for deliverance. Our Jewish friends celebrate Passover as a festival of deliverance, identifying with their forebears who were "slaves in Egypt." They were oppressed as strangers in a strange land, yet their deliverance by God opened the future for them.

This first clause about liberation leads to a reminder of the covenant God makes with Moses as the representative of Israel. Moses himself had been liberated from his guilt as a murderer (Ex. 3) in order to become God's agent for the exodus from Egypt. Troubles along the road led to the drama on Mount Sinai, where, through Moses, God gave Israel the Ten Commandments as evidence of the covenant. The preface to the Ten Commandments in

Exodus 20:2 underlines the importance of God's liberation for Israel: "I am the LORD your God who brought you out of the land of Egypt, out of the house of slavery." Deliverance is a mark of grace, a connection between God and the people God chooses. The covenant is the way of expressing gratitude to God for our deliverance, however it has come to us.

Covenant gratitude is a way of life, as the remainder of this second phrase emphasizes. The threefold description comes from Micah 6:8b. Each of the elements—doing justice, loving mercy, and walking humbly with the Lord—are hallmarks of a thankful life lived as God has taught. *Doing justice* sounds easy, until we realize that it is the disadvantaged who are least likely to be treated with justice. "Doing justice" differs from enforcing the law in that seeking to give each person his or her proper due differs from watching for infractions.

Loving mercy adds a dimension to loving justice. Those who have experienced mercy will love it out of appreciation for the difference mercy has made in their own lives. One who has become covenanted to God through deliverance will extend that same mercy to others. Mercy is something to be shared, extended. Evangelism is in fact showering those around us with the mercy God has extended to us.

The final component, *walking humbly with God* fulfills the covenant with a fellowship where God's mercy and holiness are celebrated. Covenant life must be relational, a community of those on whom God has shed mercy. When we recognize how miraculous God's gift of mercy is, it helps us to build a community where the news of God's love overflows into the world around us.

The Presbyterian Church (U.S.A.) understands itself to be just such a covenant community. There are boundaries, shared understandings of how we live out our gratitude, that some people may find peculiar. We understand that, and yet we ourselves may sometimes wonder at the diversity as well as the dynamics of our fellowship. It is a sense of a covenanted community that holds us together. As we seek to implement mission, it is essential that we never forget our roots.

A semicolon introduces the consequences of the covenant, summing up the rest of the Old Testament. "The rest of the story" is that God confronts Israel, God's own chosen people, "with the responsibilities of this covenant." *Confront* is a modern and strong word, one that suggests an in-your-face move. It is a word that grabs our attention, makes us sit up a bit straighter, wondering what will come next. There is a tendency to slow down, recognizing that God did not merely remind Israel of the terms of the covenant, but confronted Israel with them. The biblical prophets fulfilled this role, often introducing their message with "Thus says the LORD."

That prophetic message is summarized as having two equally important responsibilities that come with God's covenant. On the one hand, there is judgment for their unfaithfulness. Even this word conveys the message that there is falling short of, as well as acting against, what God requires in the covenant. As the Westminster Shorter Catechism puts it, "Sin is any want of conformity unto, or transgression of, the law of God."[24] One may fall off the bicycle either way. The discussion of the Ten Commandments in both Westminster catechisms, as well as in the Heidelberg Catechism, makes it clear that the covenant requirements in the Ten Commandments both require and forbid. The covenant can be broken both ways.

"While" continues the sentence, offering hope. The biblical prophets remind Israel that the God of the covenant also sustains the people "by divine grace." This is the aspect of the covenant that is often not understood. The covenant "works" because of God's grace, God's love for God's people. The definition of grace as "unmerited favor" suggests the mysterious wonder of God's relationship with God's people.

God's good news continues to be that God loves and cares for you and me beyond what we deserve. God reminds us in numerous ways when we stray from the path God would have us walk, and that is evidence of God's care for us. This good news is the heart of the church's mission.

What began as a lament ends with affirmation and hope. Brilliance emerges from the dark clouds of rebellion and selfishness. God's grace triumphs by coming into the lives of those who are God's people. The second section of the symphony ends in a quietly triumphant major moment of hope.

Processional (G-3.0102)

The words "God's redeeming and reconciling activity" come as a trumpet call announcing the arrival of an important dignitary. This phrase is at the heart of the Christian faith. How boldly this declaration comes! Moving past centuries of pondering how this could be, we find ourselves standing with the earliest Christians for whom these five words became the proclamation of good news.

"Was incarnate." We want to say more. Questions arise for us as the power of this announcement seeps into us. We realize that these words challenge most people who carry deep within them some understanding of what is meant by the word *God*. To affirm that God was incarnate in Jesus Christ is to make enormous claims that still shake those who hear these words today. We have come to the heart of our mission: a proclamation of five words.

Were we to say simply these words, the response would likely be, "Who is this Jesus Christ?" A response more consistent with the biblical witness would be, "What did this Jesus do?" The comma after *Christ* signals a pause for just such questions. As the church goes about its mission, questions such as these continue to remind us of the initial contention of this chapter: that our "mission is given form by God's activity in the world." The remainder of this paragraph explores what that phrase means. The foundation has been laid, since God's purpose is the same "yesterday, today, and forever." The emphasis is on what is done, as well as why it is done.

Questions such as these were forwarded to Jesus from John the Baptist when John was a prisoner. Jesus' fivefold answer reported in Matthew 11:5 and Luke 4:18–19 is the basis for the rest of the sentence. In Nazareth Jesus read from Isaiah 61:1–2, where these actions are recorded, thereby indicating the nature of his ministry. Presbyterians throughout history have listened to God's Spirit speaking in this text, and have done so as a way to conform their mission to Jesus' teaching. How to interpret these five phrases is a continuing challenge as we seek to be faithful to our Lord.

The actions of Jesus indicated in this first sentence of G-3.0102 are as follows:

- Jesus "announced good news to the poor." This is the bedrock of Christian witness. The church is in the "business" of announcing good news. Issues we face are such things as: Who are the poor? What is "good news"? How do we proclaim in a way that the poor can hear?
- Jesus "proclaimed release for prisoners." Not all prisons have stone walls. Jesus liberated those chained in hopeless situations. For every sentenced prisoner, there are multitudes caught in

nets of addictions of various sorts. How do we find those imprisoned? What is the "release" the church declares?

- "Jesus proclaimed . . . the recovery of sight to the blind." Who are the blind? What about those whose perspective on life needs the care that "opens their eyes" to other ways of managing their lives? Lack of awareness can be seen as a curable disease, as well as an overly restricted focus ignoring the context.

- "Jesus . . . let the broken victims go free." Both in Isaiah and here, there is a parallel between this action and the concern for prisoners. This action suggests that there are around us persons who are broken in spirit as well as body, who need care and healing to reenter the world of human interaction. Responding to those who are broken around us is another dimension of mission given us by our Lord.

- "Jesus proclaimed . . . the year of the Lord's favor." This last phrase is challenging. Gerhard Friedrich offers this comment as explanation:

[Jesus] proclaims, like a herald, the year of the Lord, the Messianic age. When heralds proclaimed the year of jubilee throughout the land with the sound of the trumpet, the year began, the prison doors were opened and debts were remitted. The preaching of Jesus is such a blast of the trumpet. Its result is that the Word proclaimed becomes a reality.[25]

Our mission is to continue announcing that God has fulfilled God's promise to send a messiah. Such proclamation is another aspect of telling the good news.

There is a tendency to focus on one or another of these five activities as the more critical. Having all five activities in one sentence suggests that all are important. Jesus kept a balance, so that all of these activities emerge as components of Jesus' mission. The challenge we face as we work out our mission is to find a balance for our stewardship of the mission Christ has given us.

The second sentence of G-3.0102 presents the life, death, and resurrection of Jesus and demonstrates what God's intention was for those who follow the incarnate God. The first phrase of this summary of Jesus' ministry describes him as one who "came to seek and to save the lost." This phrase comes from Luke 19:10; it was Jesus' response to those who grumbled when he went to eat with Zacchaeus. These few words remind us that Jesus was the Good

Shepherd (John 10:11), fulfilling what Ezekiel 34 had promised. We too are called to seek out those who are lost, and to offer them compassion and the words of hope and eternal life.

The second phrase summarizes Jesus' life, as prelude to his death on a cross: ". . . in his life and death for others God's redeeming love for all people was made visible."

We are brought to the cross, the center of our faith, where words suggest rather than explain. These sixteen words express our faith that Jesus' life and death make God's purpose uniquely evident. As I write this, I am keenly aware there is much else which can be said, and has been. Yet there is a sense in which allusion and suggestion are all we can do. The Confession of 1967 reminds us that "God's reconciling act in Jesus Christ is a mystery."[26]

The text focuses on mission. How do the life and death of Jesus of Nazareth inform mission? The answer we find in this phrase is that the way Jesus lived and died makes God's purpose uniquely evident. The theme of God's grace from G-3.0101 is transformed into "redeeming love" through the Son.

"Redeeming" indicates what is unique about God's love. Many of us associate this word with the chorus "I Know That My Redeemer Liveth" from Haydn's oratorio *Messiah*. Many are surprised to learn that the text comes from the Old Testament, Job 19:25. A biblical concordance indicates that "redeem" is more frequent in the Old Testament than in the New: 140 times in the former; 22 times in the latter.

Friedrich Büchsel notes that the verb *agorazo* is derived from the Greek word for commercial activity in the marketplace, especially the freeing of slaves. In 1 Corinthians 6:20 and 7:23, Paul uses the word to indicate that "Christians are not free but are the possession of Christ."[27] This may account, to some degree, for the so-called ransom theory of the atonement that arose from Paul's use of this commercial term.

Another term for "redeem," *exagorazo,* appears in Galatians 3:13 and 4:5, where the reference is also to Christ's redemption, now to freedom. Büchsel notes that Paul now uses this word as a metaphor for redemption, suggesting that Paul "sees the process [of redemption] as something which took place towards us and in our favour, not as something which took place towards God and in His favour."[28] He goes on to suggest that God, "is the One who acts in the cross of Jesus."

The *Book of Order* phrase reminds us that Jesus is the incarnation of God's love, a love that is both costly and liberating. The Confession of 1967 reminds us that "God's sovereign love is a mystery beyond the reach of man's mind."[29] While God's love is a mystery, we must proclaim the mystery, making sure that our zeal of proclamation does not limit God's initiative.

A prepositional phrase may indeed startle us when it speaks of "God's redeeming love for all people." Since we are considering our mission as Presbyterians, this phrase reminds us that the good news is to be proclaimed to all the world. The audience for which the gospel is meant is nothing less than the whole world. Our responsibility is to be stewards of this message, obedient to our Lord's command to carry this word to the "uttermost parts of the earth."

Some might find here a suggestion of "universalism," the view that in the end God will save all the world, and that thus we have no impetus for spreading the good news. From our Calvinistic and Reformed heritage, we are assured that God will save whomever God wants to. Our commitment to God's sovereign freedom (G-2.0500a) reminds us that our estimation of who is a saint is at best provisional. Chapter 27 of the Westminster Confession makes this point with its careful distinction between the visible and the invisible church.[30] The word *all* means just that. We have a universal assignment, the success or failure of which is determined by our loving and compassionate God. We are called, as the hymn puts it, to

> Lift high the cross,
> The love of Christ proclaim
> Till all the world adore
> His sacred name.[31]

The third phrase brings us to the heart of our faith, the resurrection of Jesus Christ. Since Paul wrote 1 Corinthians 15, Christians have understood the dire consequences for faith "if Christ has not been raised."[32] Here we arrive at the heart of mission. There can be no good news, no joy, no genuine hope, without the resurrection.

In answer to the question, "In what sense?" there is a two-pronged answer. On the one hand, there is "assurance of God's victory over sin and death." Assurance is the taproot of faith, the dynamic for mission. What Paul suggests in his resurrection hymn in 1 Corinthians 15 is that assurance flows from Jesus' resurrection.

In a time when there are many voices proclaiming themselves as guarantors of assurance, the account of Jesus' death and resurrection stands alone.

Sports fans know the elation of winning a game or a series or a title. There are demonstrations, parades, and other exhibitions of elation. These are celebrations of transient glory, temporary relief from the ordinary. The quest for victory in life's struggles feeds the competitive streak that often characterizes American society.

Victory for the Christian is always God's victory over "sin and death." The first war of the third millennium is called the war on terrorism. As daunting as this challenge is, it pales beside the struggle with sin and death. The resurrection is God's declaration of victory over these two enduring enemies of sin and death. You and I still sin, and we deal with death: continually with that of others, ultimately with our own. There is only one victor.

The other prong of the resurrection for us is the "promise of God's continuing presence in the world." The God who has demonstrated faithfulness continues to be present in our world, although this may not be evident. The mission of the church is not something we do as if God were far from us. God continues to be present as God has been from the beginning. Scripture reminds us that God always keeps promises made. Our mission is walking and working with God nearby, our strength and our help. Mission would be utterly impossible if we were trying to manage it on our own.

How is God present? That takes us into the finale of the first movement.

Mazurka (G-3.0103)

The mission symphony has marched along in 4/4 time until now, driving forward as Scripture's account of God's activity in the world was summarized. As we come to the final paragraph about God's activity (G-3.0103), there is a change of tone, suggesting the need for a change in tempo as we consider the Holy Spirit.

I appreciate hymns in 3/4 time in church, except for processionals. One reason is that I remember Victor Borge's line, "There will be no waltzing in the aisles, unless it is absolutely necessary." Some Presbyterians have discovered the possibility suggested in the Directory for Worship, that a pastor may chose to use "drama, dance, and other art forms"[33] as a way to "create ardor as well as order."[34] A mazurka differs from a waltz by stressing either the second or third beat in an irregular way, introducing an improvisational dimension to the music.

This provision begins restating the theme of the chapter: "God's redeeming and reconciling activity in the world." A popular phrase from politics, "staying on message," reminds us that these few words are how we Christians today can "stay on message." We are witnesses to what God has done and is doing in the world. This brief phrase is a candidate for our mission statement.

God's activity "continues through the power and presence of the Holy Spirit." The Creator continues to be both present to God's creatures and creation, not as a spectator or a remote controller, but as One who lovingly cares for all creation. God's instrumentality is the Holy Spirit, on whom we now focus.

According to this teaching, God acts through the Holy Spirit to accomplish two tasks, indicated by the two phrases in this sentence. The first verb is *confront*, a startlingly modern word popular in describing tense relationships between humans. This word grabs our attention when we see it. We wonder whether it is really an appropriate word to describe something God does. Yet this is what God did through the prophets, as noted in G-3.0101b.

God confronts "individuals and societies." The reference to Israel has become differentiated for modern readers. It is people individually and collectively. This is a contemporary way to express the prophetic function of mission, to prepare the way of the Lord. We are reminded that our faith is communal as well as personal. God continues to desire a people who discover themselves as they learn how to grow in obedience to God.

The message of confrontation is "Christ's Lordship of life," all of life. Christ is Lord of all, in the fullest possible sense of that word. Mission has a responsibility to remind all of us what it means to call Jesus Lord. Again, the scope of mission is expanded to include the "whole inhabited earth."

Christ's Lordship is of life. Jesus himself announced. "I came that they may have life, and have it abundantly."[35] Jesus defines life as God created it to be. Life is God's gift to humanity, to be used as the gift was intended.

The other verb is "call." This word plays a major role in Scripture as well as in the Presbyterian family. God called the prophets, and we believe that God calls each of us in one way or another.[36] God through the Holy Spirit calls us to service, and we decide whether and how to respond to that call.

In this chapter, God's call is "to repentance and to obedience." *Repentance* underlines our involvement in ways that are not consistent with God's will. You and I are tangled in a web made sticky by the accumulated disobedience of others, as well as by the way we have managed to complicate our own lives. *Repentance* is finally realizing that we have headed down the wrong path and need to change course. *Repentance* is coming to realize that God loves us as we are, so that we can begin to comprehend what God's intent for us is, and change our ways. God's Holy Spirit works within us as well as through others to bring us to this new and better approach to life.

That new life is one where we discover the joy and fulfillment of living in obedience to God's will. Part of the new life is working out the implications of God's will together. The challenge is to live out obedience in a way that demonstrates faithfulness to the "whole counsel of God."[37] Scripture is the unique witness to God's will. The point is clear: It is the will of God that elicits repentance and empowers obedience.

We end the first movement in a dance with God's Spirit. Life in the Spirit continues a dance moving through our lives as disciples. The Spirit is the ongoing witness of God, whose activity forms our mission. It is a holy dance, where most of us stumble through the steps as we begin to comprehend the amazing grace of God, which provides the music.

NOTES

1. The Church and Its Mission," chapter III of the Form of Government, The Constitution of the Presbyterian Church (U.S.A.), Part II (*Book of Order*).
2. Eugene Peterson, *The Message* (Colorado Springs, CO: NavPress Publishing Group, 1993), p. 402.
3. An indication that the sources are extensive is found in Walter Brueggemann, *Theology of the Old Testament* (Minneapolis: Fortress Press, 1997), p. 451 n. 5, where he offers what he considers the "most important recent exegetical studies" of this concept.
4. See *The Book of Confessions* 3.03, 4.006, 4.115, 5.034, 6.023, 7,010, 7.035, 7.127, 7.185, 10.3.

5. Ibid., 4.115.
6. Ibid., 7.127.
7. Ibid., 10.3, lines, 29–32.
8. Everett Fox, *The Five Books of Moses* (New York: Schocken Books, 1983), p. 20.
9. Ibid., p. 368.
10. G-2.0400.
11. William Placher, *The Domestication of Transcendence: How Modern Thinking about God Went Wrong* (Louisville: Westminster John Knox Press, 1996).
12. Ibid., p. 61. Quotation is from John Calvin, *Concerning the Eternal Predestination of God,* tr. J. K. S. Reid (London: James Clarke, 1961), p. 56.
13. Eugene Peterson, *The Message* (Colorado Springs, CO: Navpress, 1993), p. 402.
14. Marilynne Robinson, *The Death of Adam: Essays on Modern Thought* (New York: Houghton Mifflin Co., 1998), p. 88.
15. Ibid., pp. 88–89.
16. This vision can serve as helpful commentary on the definition of the purpose of the Church of Jesus Christ in G-3.0200.
17. Gen. 9:17.
18. G-2.0500a(1).
19. Stanley Walters, "Jacob Narrative," in David Noel Freedman, ed., *The Anchor Bible Dictionary* (New York: Doubleday, 1992), vol. 3, p. 605.
20. J. C. Beker, *Paul the Apostle* (Philadelphia: Fortress Press, 1980), p. 328. Beker cites as his source for this Peter Richardson, *Israel in the Apostolic Church,* Society for New Testament Studies Monograph Series 10 (London: Cambridge University, 1969).
21. Ibid., p. 344.
22. "When Israel Was in Egypt's Land," in *The Presbyterian Hymnal* (Louisville: Westminster/John Knox Press, 1990), no. 334.
23. Ps. 130:1.
24. *The Book of Confessions,* 7.014.
25. Gerhard Friedrich, *kēryssō,* in Gerhard Kittel, ed., *Theological Dictionary of the New Testament,* vol. 3 (Grand Rapids: Wm. B. Eerdmans Publishing Company, 1965), pp. 706–707.
26. *The Book of Confessions,* 9.09.
27. Friedrich Büchsel, *agorazō,* in Kittel, vol. 1, p. 125.
28. Ibid., p. 127.
29. *The Book of Confessions,* 9.15.
30. Ibid., C-6.140-145.

31. "Lift High the Cross," *The Presbyterian Hymnal* (Louisville: West-minster/John Knox Press, 1990), no. 371.
32. 1 Cor. 15:12–20. There are seven "ifs in these verses, which hammer home the critical importance of the resurrection.
33. W-1.4005a(5).
34. W-1.2005c.
35. John 10:10.
36. G-6.0106 outlines the threefold call to ministry in the church.
37. *The Book of Confessions,* 6.006.

2

SECOND MOVEMENT: CHURCH

Fugue (G-3.0200)

The focus of the mission symphony shifts to the Church as God's agent to continue presenting God's intent in the world. The exposition of the fugue's theme opens the second movement trumpeting its bold assertion:

> The Church of Jesus Christ is
> the provisional demonstration
> of what God intends for all of humanity.

When I quoted these words in a seminary lecture, they elicited an immediate response from a startled student: "What do you mean, 'provisional'?" I was not prepared for the question, both because of its suddenness and because of the student's immediate focus on the heart of the sentence. The use of the word *provisional* to characterize the Church seems to go against our assumptions of the permanence of the church.

This sentence concentrates what was described in G-3.0101a, how God's people in ancient times were at times unfaithful. We are reminded that the Church is in fact the new Israel. As Old Testament scholar Bernhard Anderson wrote years ago, "Those who followed Moses were a . . . variegated company, 'a mixed multitude.' " (referring to Ex. 12:38).[1] Deliverance from slavery in Egypt was insufficient to produce faithfulness. The point is that God accomplishes God's purpose through whatever means God can. When one instrumentality fails, God provides an alternate means. So the word *provisional* includes a challenge to our assumption that the church as we know it will exist as long as it provides a faithful witness to the Lord of the Church. One indication of the boldness of this declaration is how seldom this sentence is cited in our life together.

Our *Book of Confessions* reminds us how provisional the Church is. The Scots Confession wrestles with the problem of "The Notes by which the True Kirk shall be determined from the False, and who shall be judge of doctrine" (3.18). The Second Helvetic Confession devotes several paragraphs (5.124–.141) to a consideration of this dilemma, separating the Church Militant from the Church Triumphant (5.127). The Westminster Confession differentiates between the visible and invisible church, acknowledging that "the purest churches under heaven are subject both to mixture and error (6.144).

The verb *is* offers us another challenge. The Church of Jesus Christ, of which Presbyterians hope to be a part, *is* by its nature a witness, an inescapable accompaniment to our profession of faith. What you and I do as we seek to be faithful to our calling contributes, positively or negatively, to this witness. And this refers, not to any particular congregation or governing body or denomination, but to all those who claim Jesus Christ as Lord. This bold assertion reminds us of the broad fellowship we share. Our family is very large.

The apostle Paul described the Church as the body of Christ, even to the point of telling the disputatious Corinthians that "you [plural] are the body of Christ."[2] The sentence from the *Book of Order* now appears as a paraphrase of Pauline Scripture, an expression to challenge us to a larger understanding of the Church of Jesus Christ than we might otherwise hold. "Our" church is always theologically erroneous. The Church belongs only to the Lord of the Church, Jesus Christ. We are stewards of the good news, those who bear tidings of good news.

The dilemma of "provisional" is the continuing struggle from Corinth to churches in our day over how to deal with what has been called "the old Adam in the New Jerusalem."[3] We sing about this dilemma:

> Mid toil and tribulation,
> And tumult of her war,
> She waits the consummation
> Of peace forevermore;
> Till with her vision glorious,

Her longing eyes are blest,
And the great church victorious,
Shall be the church at rest.[4]

This dilemma has always been a troubling issue, one that periodically leads to disruption in church life. Our predecessors in 1789 noted that churches may err "in making the terms of communion either too lax or too narrow; yet, even in this case, they do not infringe upon the liberty or the rights of others, but only make an improper use of their own."[5] Those who come into the Presbyterian fellowship from other traditions sometimes find this attitude difficult to accept.

The "body of Christ" metaphor relates to the word *body* in terms of what a body does. The emphasis in Paul's explanations has to do with functions, with action, with what the parts of the body do. When a body part no longer functions as intended, surgeons recommend discarding that part. "Demonstrating" is what the body of Christ is called to do. As one part of the body seeks to be faithful in fulfilling its role, it shows that it is doing what it should. And the primary determiner of whether that part is faithful is the Lord of the Church, its Head.

Even more challenging is the rest of the sentence: " . . . what God intends for all of humanity." We tend to read past the subject of this phrase, when we should be brought up short. It is what **God** intends, not simply what we think or even earnestly believe God (as we understand "God") intends. When we say or read the word *God* (or any of the other references to the Ultimate Creator), perhaps we might pause for a moment, humbling ourselves in God's holy presence. It is not what you or I or someone else proclaims God's intent to be, but rather that we are preparing to "find and represent the will of Christ" (G-4.0301d). We should hear within us these words: "You shall have no other gods before me" (Ex. 20:3).

The third millennium opens as an era of many gods. Adherents of religions cry out that the "true" god is the one who calls for some specific requirement or other. In the name of a god, people are killed, suggesting that their god requires human sacrifice. Other gods are principles to which people give their ultimate devotion, zealously serving a single principle, whatever the cost.

The words of G-3.0200 might be sung or chanted, rather than read as "ordinary" text. Then some of the richness could emerge, as words and music combined to express their holy grandeur. It would emerge in a harmonic episode, evoking the scene of Isaiah in the Temple (Isa. 6).[6]

In such a world, the church is called to demonstrate what the God and Father of Jesus Christ intends for all humanity. Such an understanding of mission assumes a stance of reverent humility, in which we carefully consider how what is presented represents what the Lord God intends for all humanity. We serve God in the specifics of our lives, recognizing that our faithfulness is never completely faithful, and trusting that God uses what we do for God's purposes.

The word *gospel* is defined in terms, not of message, but of action. The Church is now demonstrating, not simply proclaiming, what God is up to. A more familiar expression is "Thy kingdom come, thy will be done on earth as it is in heaven." The familiar comment "Your actions speak so loudly that I can't hear what you say" applies to the church's responsibility.

In juxtaposition, "God" (as the One whose intention the church is to follow) and "all of humanity" combine to overwhelm the reader. While these words appear to be abstract, some reflection makes one aware of the scope and the importance of the sentence. There is a power inherent in these few words, the power for mission, a power that comes from God.

This restatement of the theme poses the question, "What is our church demonstrating about God's intention for all humanity?" The remainder of the movement, indeed the rest of chapter III, suggests the dimensions of a response. The brass timbre that opens this second movement continues to challenge as well as to inspire the church.

As if in recognition of how formidable the opening of this movement is, a restatement follows immediately:

> The Church is called to be
> a sign in and for the world
> of the new reality
> which God has made available to people in Jesus Christ.

The changes are subtle, yet this exposition is more "accessible" to our time. In the restatement, the subject is just Church, still capitalized, without the prepositional phrase. The simple verb *is* has been replaced by the compound *called to be*, which softens the impact further. Changing the verb from *is* to *called* with the infinitive, *to be*, signals that the church we know is pressing on to the mark of the high calling in Jesus Christ.[7] "Provisional demonstration" is rephrased as "to be a sign in and for the world." "What God intends" becomes "the new reality which God has made available . . . in Jesus Christ." For all of humanity is now "to people."

Each theme stands alone, without losing any of the power inherent in either statement. We wonder why there are two statements that are so similar. One possible answer is to appeal to people who have different ways of thinking. When I have shown both statements to elders without indicating the source, their responses indicated whether each person preferred abstract or concrete statements.

The "new reality" is presented in a way that is multidimensional. The new reality is revealed in Jesus Christ, called in Scripture "the kingdom of God." Such a "new reality" is not the result of human inquiry. It is a fulfillment of God's promise to do a "new thing" (Isa. 43:19). It is the sort of newness Jesus described in the parable of new cloth and new wine in all three Gospels (Matt. 9:16–17; Mark 2:21–22; Luke 5:36–39). Good news is rooted in an understanding of God's "new thing" coming to us in the birth, life, death, and resurrection of Jesus Christ.

This second development continues with three episodes, each beginning with "new." These are not simply nice ideas from some theologian, but are described as hallmarks of what Jesus Christ has revealed about God's intent. As we look at these three phrases, we might imagine that they are voices in a fugue, where the three component phrases interact and interweave in contrapuntal ways, producing through this interweaving an effect beyond simple melody. The source of this joyous fugue may well be 2 Cor. 5:16–21. For Paul for those who are in Christ, "everything has become new" (2 Cor. 5:17b). A fitting hymn as background for this fugue, in tempo and tune, if not text, would be "I Danced in the Morning."[8]

The first phrase is "the new humanity." This expression rephrases a theme of the first movement: that God called to God's self a people with a purpose of obeying God's intent for creation. This way of referring to "the Church" extends the notion of church many of us carry in our heads.

"A new humanity": what an intriguing thought! Perhaps God's work is creating a new humanity to fulfill God's creative purpose, to demonstrate that there is a way humankind can go about living that celebrates God's goodness and power. In a world where "transform" is a buzzword, here is an intimation that what God intends for humankind is totally new, totally different than any understanding of how the human race might get along with one another.

When the United Nations was formed in 1948, two groups soon formed. One might be called the party of fear, those who challenged "one worldism," lamenting the loss of national sovereignty to be replaced by dreamers who would ruin the "more advanced" countries in their drive to make all people equal. The other group, the party of hope, envisaged a world freed from the horrors of international war and able to spread human rights to all humanity. Fifty-five years later, we now know that neither prediction was correct. The new humanity motif sounds a note of hope, while recognizing that God's kingdom cannot be constructed simply from human good intentions but must come through the transforming love of God in Jesus Christ.

The second phrase is "a new creation." If the suggestion of a new humanity is broad, this second phrase goes well beyond the first. These three words remind me of the vision in Revelation 21:1, where John writes, "Then I saw a new heaven and a new earth." This vision may seem threatening or ominous to many. The prospect of massive change, a new creation, gives us pause. We begin to think of what we would miss, and we find ourselves grieving for the world we live in. A friend who moved to another country as an adult discovered that assumptions that had worked well throughout her life were now no longer useful. To contemplate the possibility of a new reality is even more daunting.

Such a human, "natural" reaction reminds us of how human we are, in the old sense. We prefer what we know, more than trusting the Creator who will again create all things and make them consistent with the love and grace we know in our Savior Jesus Christ. Why then do we pray so often, "Thy kingdom come"? To mean that three-word phrase is to yearn for the renewal of creation, which presently only reveals the "labor pains" of the kingdom, as Paul puts it in Romans 8:22.

There is a challenge inherent in this phrase: Do we trust God with a new creation? The Madison Avenue Presbyterian Church in New York City has as its invitation on the radio an indication that coming to church "could change everything." Are we ready to let loose of what we hold dear, of what we consider our accomplishments, our status, our "net worth," however we reckon it? From time to time, it is well to ask ourselves whether we are ready for God's new creation, and to pause before we pray, "Thy kingdom come." The third phrase of G-3.0200b is longer, capping the other two, beginning to shift from "what" to "how." This phrase is: "a new beginning for human life in the world." After the challenges of the first two phrases, the shift to "beginning" is a word of grace.

It is yet another reminder of G-3.0100, the "holy history" of God's purpose for creation. That story is, in essence, a story of new beginnings. God's faithfulness becomes Divine persistence, starting over time and again when God's people fall short of the Plan. Creation, Abraham, Moses, the prophets, Jesus all represent divine do-overs, indications of God's gracious intent for all of creation.

This third "new" is an inclusive "beginning" for nothing less than "all human life." Furthermore, this inclusive beginning is "for life in the world." Such a do-over relates to persons, and communities, and ultimately to reality itself. This third phrase ends with a colon rather than a period, a grace note that introduces three sequences or hallmarks that characterize this new beginning. These marks are not proposed as new, but as reminders of the scope and purpose of mission as presented in Scripture.

The order of these marks indicates that they are to be taken as a "package," not divided into some priority or chronological order. We have come upon an apparently simple yet comprehensive description of what the rule or kingdom of God would include. These three are as interrelated as other listings we find in this chapter. One implication is that these three marks become ways of determining how well the Church is demonstrating what God intends for all humanity.

The first sign is this: "Sin is forgiven." A challenge at the end of Jesus' ministry concerned his authority to forgive sins (Matt. 21:23–27 and parallels). Jesus responded with another question, this one about John the Baptist. We regularly pray in the Lord's Prayer, "Forgive us our debts, as we forgive our debtors." But we forget the next two verses:

> For if you forgive others their trespasses, your heavenly Father will also forgive you; but if you do not forgive others, neither will your Father forgive your trespasses.[9]

Forgiveness is at the heart of Christian discipleship. Were it not for God's gracious forgiveness, which allows for second chances, none of us would have the hope and strength for discipleship.

The second indicator is this: "Reconciliation is accomplished." We Presbyterians produced an official understanding of the implications of 2 Corinthians 5:10 that we call the Confession of 1967. The Confession in its opening paragraph declares:

> He [Jesus Christ] is present in the church by the power of the Holy Spirit to continue and complete his mission. This work of God, the Father, Son, and Holy Spirit, is the foundation of all confessional statements about God, [humanity], and the world. Therefore, the church calls [us] to be reconciled to God and to one another.[10]

The Confession is divided into three parts, indicating how Presbyterians understand the ministry of reconciliation:

- Part I   God's Work of Reconciliation
- Part II   The Ministry of Reconciliation
- Part III   The Fulfillment of Reconciliation

Part II, where the first section is titled "The Mission of the Church," begins with the sentence, "To be reconciled to God is to be sent into the world."[11] Edward Dowey commented on this sentence as follows:

> The force of the entire Confession is in this short expression. The first phrase, to be reconciled to God, is a concentrated summary of Part I. The last part of the sentence, to be sent into the world as his reconciling community, epitomizes Part II. The verb *is* holds them together like the pin in a hinge.[12]

Dowey's hardware metaphor seems to clash with our musical theme, yet puts the relationship in plain language.

The final hallmark is this: "The dividing walls of hostility are torn down," a phrase from Ephesians 2:14. Paul reminds the church in Ephesus that they were considered foreigners to God's covenant promise, since they were Gentiles. This wall of separation between peoples has been removed through the life, death, and resurrection of Jesus Christ. The previous hostility between two separate peoples has been "put to death." Jesus is the door to a new humanity where division and separation are overcome. This text emphasizes that overcoming hostility is the key to becoming a new community that can share the message of reconciliation.

These last three themes of forgiven sin, accomplished reconciliation, and demolished dividing walls form a counterpoint moving to a cadence, where the hallmarks dance with one another until there is a larger whole. Such interplay is integral to a Presbyterian sense of mission in the twenty-first century.

Yet the interplay of these three hallmarks has proven difficult for the Church, and particularly the Presbyterian branch. Many seem unaware of this distressing history. As recently as 1983, two branches on the Presbyterian tree celebrated their reuniting when the Presbyterian Church in the United States and the United Presbyterian Church in the United States of America became the Presbyterian Church (U.S.A.) at a General Assembly meeting in Atlanta, Georgia. Their division, dating from 1861, was caused by a dispute related to the outbreak of the Civil War.

That division was foreshadowed by the Old School/New School division in 1837, arising from numerous disputes concerning mission and theology. Prior to that controversy was the bitter Old Side/New Side division, which lasted from 1741 to 1757. At that time, issues of who could become a candidate for ministry, whether a minister could preach in the parish of another installed minister, and how the church's mission was to be funded combined to separate the two Presbyterian wings.

These have been the major events in our history. Throughout this history Presbyterians have used harsh language with one another that escalated into divisions and separations. For example, the reunion period in the 1980s also saw the formation of the Presbyterian Church in America and the Evangelical Presbyterian Church, groups that preferred to separate from the major bodies rather than continue with those with whom they could not in good conscience continue to serve.

The three interrelated characterizations of Christ's "new reality" in G-3.0200b challenge contemporary Presbyterians to learn from our past, rather than continue our fractious ways. We are all called to grow, to consider with great reverence and care whether we are in fact answering the summons of the Lord of the Church to "build up the body of Christ." Will we learn to dance the fugue of faith?

G-3.0200c comes as encouragement and challenge, a trumpet call ringing through the complexity with another call, presenting a third way of defining the church: "The Church *is* the body of Christ, both in its corporate life and in the lives of its individual members, and is called to give shape and substance to this truth."

This definition returns to the first definition (G-3.0200) by repeating the verb *is* in its strong form. "The Church *is* the body of Christ." This sentence is the culmination of the section. Listening to an unfamiliar symphony, one senses that the movement is coming to a climax, where the various strains are meeting for a climactic expression. This sentence has that quality.

"Both" reminds us that as it claims to be the body of Christ, the Church consists of two dimensions, one in "its corporate life" and one "in the lives of its individual members." The body of Christ is about life. Otherwise, it would be merely an antiquarian curiosity, a museum piece.

This phrase evokes a memory of how my father and I debated this issue at table, usually on Sunday after church. Dad understood "church" to be a collection of individual Christians, each of whom bore responsibility for living faithfully according to the Bible. It seemed to me that somehow, the church was more than the sum of its members. We were never able to find a resolution, other than to accept that this was a point on which we differed. That discussion continues in many forms today.

On the one hand, the corporate life of the church presents a witness for or against the good news of Jesus Christ. In a comment responding to a request regarding a session borrowing from a restricted fund for a purpose other than the object for which they were given, the Advisory Committee on the Constitution commented:

> Quite apart from obligations placed upon a governing body or congregation by civil law; the church lives in the world as a witness to Jesus Christ. Honesty, transparency, and trustworthiness must mark our dealings with one another (G-10.0102i).[13]

How the church does this sort of witnessing is always a delicate matter. The central issue boils down to the well-known maxim "Actions speak louder than words." At the same time, actions are ambiguous; they can be understood in various ways.

The actions of the General Assembly, indeed of all governing bodies, are taken in a variety of ways. Positions taken and statements adopted for guidance are understood as representing how Presbyterians understand a particular social or economic issue. Continuing publicity that such actions are intended as guidance fails to assuage the hurt of those who have a different position.

The issue of how corporate witness and personal witness are related to each other lies close to the bone of the "troubles" to which we Presbyterians are heirs. Like the other paradoxes that emerge in our *Book of Order*,[14] how to understand and deal with divergent personal and corporate views and behaviors is an issue every one of us needs to wrestle with and resolve in one way or another. Nor is this a recent development. Indeed, such a tension lies at the heart of all our social relationships. One evidence of the humanness of the church is this tension, reminding us that "provisional demonstration" restrains us from premature idealism about our beloved church. The importance of "conscience" for Presbyterians indicates the importance of this struggle, and an appreciation that different people will choose alternate paths in their discipleship.[15]

Such choices are difficult, painful, and finally unavoidable. Facing these uncomfortable alternatives is the high price we put on the significance of both personal values and corporate membership. Other religious bodies have chosen other ways of negotiating this human paradox, which is their right.[16]

Complicating this paradox is the diversity of our denomination. Many Presbyterians are relatively unaware of this dimension of our church. When I worked for the denomination, I found that many people understood only that I worked "for the presbytery." Many pastors serve throughout their ministries within a particular presbytery or synod. Yet a unique possibility for our ministers is to be considered as a candidate for pastor in any church in the entire denomination. Recently, this has been expanded to include as well the Evangelical Lutheran Church in America, the Reformed Church in America, and the United Church of Christ.

There is geographical diversity. When people move from one region of the country to another, they discover that the Presbyterian church in their new area differs from the one they left. Commissioners to the General Assembly are sometimes astounded at the ethnic, geographical, and theological diversity of their fellow commissioners. It is often said that there are as many ways of being a presbytery as there are presbyteries.

The final phrase of G-3.0200c restates the point of the previous material. It asserts that the church "is called to give shape and substance to this truth." "This truth" is the Church as the body of Christ. How often do we hear the question, "How come the Church has done this?" The challenge all of us face is the need, in word and deed, in style as well as content, to testify that we are seeking to fulfill God's purpose for all humanity. We are painfully aware that we will fall short. Yet we keep on growing, seeking to be faithful to our calling.

Once, when I identified myself as a Presbyterian, a person from another denomination remarked, "Oh, you're one of those structural fundamentalists." We Presbyterians have, over the last thirty years or so, spent a great deal of time, energy, and money on what we call our structure. "Structure" has replaced "order" as our key concern. "Structure" is understood as what "shape" means in the phrase under consideration. "Structure" brings with it assumptions and connotations that confuse and confound our sense of being the body of Christ. "Structure" feeds the comment that, after all, the church is just another social organization.

"Shape" has a more organic and dynamic sense, more appropriate to Paul's notion that it is in the functioning that the Church is the body of Christ. Components of the physical structure of the body—bones, muscles, veins and arteries, organs, and so forth—are under the surface, serving how the person goes about living and doing. Becoming focused on structure without an accompanying sense of whose we are, and who is the Lord of the church, suggests that we have begun to depart from our faith commitment to the mission to which we are called. We give shape and substance, and thus are responsible for the ways in which the church goes about its business.

The *Book of Order* describes the Church of Jesus Christ as the body of Christ, offering three "definitions" of the Church in terms of its mission. Each of these offers a developing sense of how to understand the function of the Church in a general way. The inclusion of the word "called" in the final phrase introduces what becomes the major emphasis of the rest of the symphony.

NOTES

1. *Understanding the Old Testament* (Englewood Cliffs, NJ: Prentice-Hall, 1975), p. 75.
2. 1 Corinthians 12:27. This chapter presents Paul's extensive discussion of the metaphor.
3. This was a frequent comment of the late Professor Norman Victor Hope in his church history classes at Princeton Theological Seminary.

4. Samuel John Stone, "The Church's One Foundation," *The Presbyterian Hymnal* (Louisville: Westminster/John Knox Press, 1990), no. 442.

5. G-1.0302.

6. The tune of "Holy God, We Praise Your Name," in *The Presbyterian Hymnal* (no. 460), offers an appropriate setting.

7. Phil. 3:12b.

8. Sydney Carter, "I Danced in the Morning," set to the shaker tune "Simple Gifts"; *The Presbyterian Hymnal* (no. 302).

9. Matt. 6:14–15.

10. "Confession of 1967," *The Book of Confessions*, 9.07. Inclusive Language Text.

11. Ibid., 9.31.

12. Edward A, Dowey, Jr., *A Commentary on the Confession of 1967 and Introduction to "The Book of Confessions"* (Philadelphia: Westminster Press, 1968), 112. Italics added.

13. *Minutes of the 213th General Assembly* (2001), Part I, *Journal* (Louisville: Office of the General Assembly, 2001), paragraph 16.027, p. 153.

14. See W. E. Chapman, *History and Theology in the Book of Order* (Louisville: Witherspoon Press, 1999), where the tensions or paradoxes of G-1.0300 are analyzed.

15. See G-1.0301a, b; see also G-6.0108a, b, and especially the footnote.

16. Note especially G-1.0302, which might be called an ecclesiastical version of the religion clause of the First Amendment to the United States Constitution.

3

THIRD MOVEMENT: CALLED

Chorale (G-3.0300)

This movement features a new key word, one that thus far has been only implicit. That word is "called."

Presbyterians use the word "call" in multiple ways in the *Book of Order*.[1] "Call" is our Presbyterian way of reminding ourselves of God's call to humanity. There is inherent in this verb-become-noun a requirement that someone listens and hears God's call, and decides to obey the call.

It is critically important that we recognize a major shift beginning with G-3.0300, where "call" becomes the primary verb. The verb continues to be "is called," a way of emphasizing the One who calls as the Holy God. There is also the implicit question "Is anyone listening? Will anyone obey?"

As we enter the next section of the mission symphony, remember that for every "call" in the text (three in this movement, two in the next), we are invited to listen, to "pay attention," with a focus and devotion worthy of our commitment to Jesus Christ. Each "call" is a summons, a challenge to decide whether to heed the call, then how to respond.

God's call to mission is the subject of this chorale. As a choir soon learns, it is when the words are set to music that we are able to sing to God's glory. Melodic line combines with rhythm to add depth to words alone.

There are three sections to the third movement. Each section begins with the subject, "The church is called to . . . " Three different verbs introduce the three strands of mission: "tell," "present," and "be," further complicated by another three verbs, the last of which introduces five more verbs! The delineation of mission thus involves eleven dynamic processes, interacting with one another. This complex structure alerts us to the complexity of mission, suggesting also that we are summoned by God to reflect God's glorious divine, holy purpose.

One final comment as we consider G-3.0300: How important is the order of the various dimensions of mission? There is a human tendency to assume that the first item in a sequence is the most important. In the case of these aspects of mission, I suggest that we reserve judgment. Other than the division of the material, there are no indications in the text that this is more than a list. I further propose that each of us find our own sense of which items speak to us more urgently than the others. The diversity of gifts given the body of Christ suggests that the best way to begin this consideration is to follow John's comment to the various churches to which he wrote: "Let anyone who has an ear listen to what the Spirit is saying to the churches."[2]

The first statement of what the Church is called to do begins in this way:

> The Church is called to tell
> the good news of salvation
> by the grace of God through faith in Jesus Christ as the only
>   Savior and Lord,
> proclaiming in Word and Sacrament that . . .

This appears straightforward at first glance, something we have heard before. Some may be surprised to find such "traditional" material at the beginning of the list.

"Called to tell." What an interesting juxtaposition of words! It's what happens in the gospels. Matthew 9:27–31 records how two blind men are given their sight and can't keep quiet about it, even when Jesus has "sternly ordered them, 'See that no one knows of this.'" These two men have the urge to tell about their new life. The "good news" has to be shared, the joy passed around, the infectious happiness spread.

The key element of good news is "grace," God's unearned favor. Grace is the subject of the first movement, how God has from the beginning sought a people. Grace is God's persistence in God's purpose even when there is rebellion from those God loves. The theme of God's quest throughout history is the story of salvation through grace. You and I know this through the faith of others who have told us the story, helped us to hear the words and music of God's amazing grace, which comes through faith in God's only Son, Jesus Christ, our Savior and Lord.

The Church is God's storyteller, the entity that continues to proclaim the story "in Word and Sacrament." The phrase "in Word and Sacrament" indicates both the what and the how of the proclamation. Many assume that "Word" signifies the verbal witness. Presbyterian usage builds on the understanding behind G-2.0200, that Jesus Christ is the Word of God. The Scriptural basis for this is the first chapter of the Gospel of John. There is a chain of witness to "the Word incarnate": Scripture, confessions, churches, ministers, members. The relations of ministers and members is clarified in chapters 5 and 6 of the *Book of Order* (Form of Government), especially in G-6.0101:

> All ministry in the Church is a gift from Jesus Christ. Members and officers alike serve mutually under the mandate of Christ who is the chief minister of all. His ministry is the basis of all ministries; the standard for all offices is the pattern of the one who came "not to be served but to serve." (Matt. 20:28)

The inclusion of "Sacrament" offers a reminder that our witness to Jesus Christ needs always to include a mysterious dimension that goes beyond words. Baptism and Communion are aspects of our witness that are essential for church life, and that the church administers as obeying Jesus' commands.

For those who may not have ready access to G-6.0101, two subheadings come along to sketch out the intent of this provision. The first, " . . . that the new age has dawned," is to be taken in terms of its biblical meaning, not as it is popularly used in the sense of crystals and vague spirituality, nor as synonymous with the sense of the Age of Aquarius. It refers back to what we read earlier, that " . . . in the resurrection of Jesus Christ there is the assurance of God's victory over sin and death and the promise of God's continuing presence in the world" (G-3.0102). We hear the echo of 2 Corinthians 5:17: "If anyone is in Christ, there is a new creation: everything old has passed away; see, everything has become new!" We call this "good news" as proclaiming that now Jesus Christ is

Lord of all, appearances to the contrary notwithstanding. This first subhead should be scored for full organ with all stops open, resounding throughout the Church.

The second vocal entrance is longer, more complex, providing more specific content for this proclamation. The basic idea is that "God . . . is still at work in the world." The church assures people through its proclamation that the dramatic progression of the two previous movements continues. The beat goes on. This affirmation with the sweep of biblical history establishes the Presbyterian Church as connected with God's people throughout world history.

Continuity, however, can be either static or dynamic. Lest anyone reading this passage think that God is no longer relevant, no longer active, we find five expressions of what God has been and continues to do, modeling what a faithful church is called to include in its people mission:

God creates life. God who is the Creator of all things continues the work of creation through giving life to all creation. God's creativity is an ongoing characteristic of God, not a mere historic "once for all" deed. Life goes on, because God is God of the living, the One from whom life comes.

God frees those in bondage. The Old Testament testifies to God's liberation of God's people time and again. The most dramatic examples are delivering the children of Israel from slavery in Egypt through the Reed Sea and providing for their return to Jerusalem after their exile into Mesopotamia. We discussed earlier how G-3.0101b summarizes God's liberating activity.

God forgives sin. The third work of God in this presentation is central to our understanding of God. While many understand God as the One who punishes and condemns sinners, we affirm that God is the One who forgives sin. Many consider that God's basic function is to judge sin and punish sinners. The gospel is that the God who is sinned against is the God who forgives, whose basic nature is grace and love. When one has not been forgiven, one's life is in bondage and hence less than God intends.

God reconciles brokenness. God's description of creation in Genesis 1, is consistently that it is good. Yet much of the narrative of the Old Testament is about how what has been created becomes broken and twisted. We saw in chapter 1 how humans broke community with their Maker. God is the One who is able to reconcile enemies, to bridge estrangement, to repair breaks and breaches which appear impossible to mend. There is a cost for such repair work, namely, the cross. God is willing to reconcile.

God makes all things new. God is a living God, Creator and still creating. There are new things under the sun. Extrapolations from what has happened before err in omitting the possibility of God's creativity. The New Testament closes with God creating a new heaven and a new earth (Rev. 21:1). Thus, God is the One who surprises, the One who can never be counted out, the One who never gives up.

These five divine activities provide both an agenda for mission and a template for style for a church seeking to be faithful to the God of the church. These five motifs will emerge again and again in this movement of the mission symphony, elaborated and developed. This articulation of these motifs reminds us of the First Movement, as well as restating the basic understanding: that what the Church calls mission is grounded in its identity as the body of Christ, its role as God's co-worker.

The Church is called to cooperate with God, to work with God in anything and everything God intends for the fulfillment of God's ultimate Lordship of all. We as disciples are summoned to be about God's business, as the young Jesus responded to his parents (Luke 2:49b KJV). God's work will come to fruition, whether we respond positively or not.

The second statement of what the Church is called to do seems short compared to the first, yet again has three parts:

> The Church is called
> to present the claims of Jesus Christ,
> leading persons to repentance,
> acceptance of him as Savior and Lord,
> and new life as his disciples.

The infinitive is no longer *to tell* but *to present*. God's call to the Church moves beyond telling to showing, demonstrating—the dimension suggested in G-3.0200c. Mission is more than telling. "Present the claims" is a way of expressing the dimension of witnessing to the message of good news, moving beyond narrative to advocacy.

Three *claims* of Jesus Christ are outlined in this brief yet potent sentence. As some of our fellowship put it, "It's not just talking the talk; it's walking the walk." A presbytery executive revealed that he has one concern when a candidate approaches the presbytery to become a pastor: "Can this person say, 'Jesus is my Savior and my Lord'?" Until we accept the claims of Jesus Christ on our own lives, we cannot advocate that others do it.

The three clauses in G-3.0303b explain Christ's claims and outline an understanding of coming to faith. The first claim is *repentance*. The Heidelberg Catechism provides us with a two-part definition of true repentance. Step one, "the dying of the old self," is "Sincere sorrow over our sins and more and more to hate them and to flee from them."[3] What is implied here, and generally forgotten, is that repentance is what God offers as part of God's grace. Neither you nor I can on our own bring others to repentance. God alone provides the grace and gratitude necessary for repentance.

Step two, "the birth of the new self," according to Heidelberg, is "Complete joy in God through Christ and a strong desire to live according to the will of God in all good works."[4] Complete joy may be difficult to experience, but increased joy is one mark of repentance, indicating that the load that has weighed us down is gone. A strong desire is the other mark of repentance deeply experienced and more readily observed.

After repentance, the second claim of Christ to be presented is *acceptance of him as Savior and Lord*. This is why persons who desire to become members of a Presbyterian church are asked, "Who is your Lord and Savior?" The expected answer is, "Jesus Christ is my Lord and Savior." To accept Jesus Christ as Savior arises from the conviction that we are indeed forgiven through the life, death, and resurrection of Jesus Christ, and claiming that benefit. It is accepting the gracious gift offered us.

To accept Jesus as Lord is to make the theological statement that Jesus is divine. The King James Bible and other Bibles are careful to print this title in capital letters, LORD, to stand for the name God claims, in the conversation with Moses at the burning bush (Ex. 3:14–15), as the Divine Name.[5] Accepting this sacred title for Jesus affirms that Jesus is divine, truly God. It is taking to heart the assertion in John's Gospel regarding Jesus as the Word who, with God from the beginning, "was God" (John 1:1). It is tragic that so few church members are aware of the grandeur and importance of this confession of faith.

The concluding claim of Jesus Christ to be presented is "*new life as [Jesus'] disciples*." The New Testament narratives tell how the disciples moved gradually into their new life as fishers of people. The learning curve of the Twelve was not a simple curve, but one that twisted and turned as they followed Jesus. Perhaps the newness itself presented the challenge to these Galileans. To the very end, they were still struggling to figure out what Jesus was up to. It is not until after Jesus' resurrection and the gift of God's Spirit that the disciples discovered new life as a dynamic witness to God's power.

G-3.0303b is an interlude in the three-step presentation of what the Church is called to do. It seems to me that these three lines offer a presentation of Christian life distilled from the New Testament. Evangelism is a word that troubles Presbyterians. Here in the *Book of Order* we are given a simple, readily understood proposal that evangelism is presenting the claims of Jesus Christ to those around us. You and I are called to be witnesses to this, presenting claims that we ourselves have accepted. Were we to take these lines to heart, perhaps each of us would discover how to present these claims on the basis of what we have discovered in our own walk of faith.

The text of G-3.0300c initially looks much like the a and b statements. This statement follows the previous two in beginning, "The church is called to . . . " This time *tell* and *present* change to *be*. The list of activities that are usually associated with mission now is followed by a longer section describing what is involved in being "Christ's faithful evangelist."

Some ask, "What else can there be? To be the Church is to do what has been described, to obey God's call to tell and present the claims." Such a reaction is honest and understandable, in a culture where the emphasis is more on doing than being. Yet mission requires that the faithful church must also *be* as well as *do*, according to the *Book of Order*. As we have already seen: "The Church is called to be a sign in and for the world."[6]

Many disputes among Presbyterians throughout our history have dealt with what a church is supposed to be. The issue since at least 1730 has often been cast as the question, "How holy must the church, its members and officers, be?" The Westminster Confession indicates that "the purest churches under heaven are subject both to mixture and error,"[7] citing as scriptural warrant Matthew 13:24–30, Jesus' parable of the weeds in the wheat.[8] We seek to be faithful, recognizing that none of us may assume the task of cleansing the Church of mixture and error. God alone through Jesus Christ is able to purify the Church. What seems to you or me as departures from what we would desire are not warrants for us to engage in a major enterprise ridding the church of error. As someone has written, "If you find a perfect church, join it; realizing that as soon as you do, it will be less than it was."

The Church is called to be faithful, "participating in God's activity in the world . . . " This phrase reminds us that this chapter (G-3.0100 and G-3.0200) began with a review of what God has been doing, as told in the Bible. We are invited now to translate that holy story into action. The witness is to what God has done and continues to do. "Witness" must be consonant with the whole counsel of God's Word.

The method of witness is through its life for others. Words are part of witness, but only part. It is the degree to which the Church's life conforms to its destiny as the body of Christ, as it lives out Jesus' ministry (G-3.0102) in how it relates to the world around it, that the Church's faithfulness is gauged. It is so much easier to speak or write or debate, to clarify and expand and develop ideas, than it is to act in ways that can be understood as "for others." Yet the *Book of Order,* with its discussion of mission, sounds again the trumpet call to action.

Five areas of mission as witness are suggested. At this point, the chorale turns into a quintet of various instruments playing together, yet each one making its distinctive sound. Ultimately, the group blends together in a finale where the contributions meld into a glorious statement. The initial agreement has to do with technical matters, such as tune, key, length, and sequence of solos, and who is the key in terms of setting the tempo. The result, when there is harmony among the players, is superior to what any one of them could do alone.

These five dimensions of mission are those around which controversy swirls. The tendency to rank all the aspects into an order of relative importance results in establishing a competition for the attention and resources of our church. Although the nineteenth-century doctrine of the spirituality of the church was discarded long ago, its effect continues to disrupt the witness of the Presbyterian Church. The five dimensions of mission challenge that orientation from the perspective of faithfulness to what it is God has been doing, and continues doing, based on Scripture.

Healing and reconciling and binding up wounds (G-3.0300c
(3), line a)

These three caring activities emerge directly from what we know
about Jesus' ministry from the Bible. Jesus has often been called the
Great Physician, because of the many accounts of his healings in the
Gospels. Jesus sent out disciples "to heal."[9] Luke 9:6 reports that the
disciples "went through the villages, bringing the good news and
curing diseases everywhere." Acts 3:1–10 tells how Peter continued
the ministry of healing after Pentecost. To engage in healing is firmly
connected to our Christian faith. Faithful disciples are healers.

The ancient Hippocratic oath begins, "First, do no harm." The
healing ministry does well to obey this pre-Christian injunction.
Christians throughout our history have sponsored and equipped
hospitals. The connection between healing and Christian faith is
generally accepted.

The end of this line, "binding up wounds," recalls the parable
of the Good Samaritan as well as the experience of the disciples
noted above. The phrase combined with "reconciling" suggests that
these three terms refer to more than physical ailments. Since September 11, 2001, when the Twin Towers in New York City were
attacked and demolished by two airplanes, we are keenly aware of
the emotional as well as the physical wounds that people carry with
them, and that need attention. What appears to be an item on a list
of things to do becomes a direction for mission. The Church is
called to be compassionate and caring for all sorts of damages those
around us suffer.

We may use "reconcile" in an ordinary way, particularly when
we get a bank statement and wonder whether our checkbook nota-
tions are consistent with the bank's figure. That monthly chore
means that I correct my balance to agree with what the bank statement indicates my balance should be. I make some changes, so that
my checkbook is reconciled with the bank. One may choose not to
reconcile monthly. The only penalty is when the bank begins asking
for the necessary funds to replenish the account, and charges a fee
for this extra service.

Friedrich Büchsel, in his discussion of the Greek word Paul
chooses for "reconcile," notes that inherent in the word is an element of change. He notes that Paul underlines the radical change
involved, "not merely in the [human] disposition, . . . but in the

total state of [human] life."[10] The reconciled person "is a person who is visited by the love of God and who is thus awakened to love."[11] Büchsel notes that reconciliation comes as a gift, comes as love to each person in such a way that the appropriate response is also love, which becomes something to be shared. The ministry of reconciliation (2 Cor. 5:18) becomes a "kindling of love,"[12] the thankful sharing of God's living justification of the unworthy. Reconciliation becomes both message and method, the spreading of a gospel of God's love. Büchsel summarizes this ministry of content and style:

> Through the revelation of the super-abounding love of God which did not find the sacrifice of the Son too great, and which does not regard it as too humiliating to plead with [humans], we are renewed in the total state of our life.[13]

The insertion of reconciliation reminds us that faithful mission is mission that is consistent with how God in Christ has reconciled the world, that justification is the consequence of God's undeserved, unearned grace. Or, as the Confession of 1967 puts it, "This community, the church universal, is entrusted with God's message of reconciliation and shares his labor of healing the enmities which separate [humans] from God and from each other."[14]

> Ministering to the needs of the poor, the sick, the lonely, and the powerless (G-3.0300c (3), line b)

Mission is now also involved in ministering, serving. This wording echoes G-1.0307, where we are reminded by our eighteenth-century predecessors that "all church power is ministerial and declarative." Some Americans are surprised to learn that the word *minister* as used in Old World governments indicates a person authorized to act in the name of the sovereign or head of state. We Presbyterians need to remember that all who minister are required to be faithful to the style and content of the One in whose name they are ministering.

The subtle surprise in line b is that the direction of ministering is "to the needs . . . " This is consistent with line a, yet it adds a level of specificity reminding us that the needs are the priority here. Mission for Presbyterians has an aspect that focuses on those in need. The needs are human conditions of stress and hopelessness.

Line b is a distilled form of Matthew 25:31–46, where it is those who are hungry or thirsty, strangers, the sick, prisoners, and the naked that offer opportunities for ministry. These opportunities are also where we find the face of Christ. Responding to such as these in need is the message Jesus gives us. Such mission has always been a hallmark of Presbyterian mission wherever such conditions can be found. We are reminded that our Lord directs us to be aware of those whose needs are not taken seriously by others around us.[15]

"The poor, the sick, the lonely, and the powerless" is a list of human beings in trouble. The Old Testament tells us that a mark of faithfulness for God's people has been how God's people treat "widows and orphans," as well as "the stranger [alien] within the gates of the city" (for example, Deut. 10:18–19). Line b reminds us in its brevity that people of faith are called to be exemplars of compassion who understand that ministering to those in need is part of our calling. The reason for this, as G-3.0300c(3) puts it, is Scripture's witness that this is a part of "God's activity in the world."

> Engaging in the struggle to free people from sin, fear, oppression, hunger, and injustice. (G-3.0300c (3), line c)

At the third of the five ways we are called to mission, we come to what today is called "advocacy." The Presbyterian view once called "the spirituality of the church" has persisted as reluctance to speak out against "oppression, hunger, and injustice," which involves dealing with civil and political issues. America's turmoil since the 1960s has triggered a strong reaction against such struggles, which are seen as "social protest." Advocacy has often been characterized as evidence of radical politics opposed to the American way. The result has been nearly fifty years of controversy within our fellowship. Opposition to advocacy as an aspect of mission has taken many forms, with varying degrees of intensity throughout American Presbyterian history.

Here we find in our *Book of Order* a call to participate with God in a struggle to free people from five bondages. Before we dismiss this line (c) we might turn to the book of Exodus, where God calls Moses to be God's agent for the liberation of Israel from the oppression of Egypt (Ex. 3:7–12). The Old Testament has numerous testimonies of God's struggling to free Israel from oppression. This is the heritage behind the inclusion of the reminder that mission includes struggles with what many see simply as social ills.

Human conditions of *fear, oppression, hunger,* and *injustice* seen with eyes of faith are seen as evidence of *sin*. As the Confession of 1967 puts it:

The reconciling act of God in Jesus Christ exposes the evil in [humans] as sin in the sight of God. In sin, [humans] claim mastery over their own lives, turn against God and their fellow [humans], and become exploiters and despoilers of the world. They lose their humanity in futile striving and are left in rebellion, despair, and isolation.[16]

Our faith gives us eyes to see dimensions of the human condition beyond what appear to others as simply social, political, and economic issues. Our mission may at times seem to duplicate what is done by others who are motivated by human compassion. Cooperative projects undertaken with those whose motivations may differ from ours offer opportunities for us as people of faith to extend our resources. However, we must remain clear that our faith offers a depth of concern that comes from faith in Jesus Christ.

People serving in food pantries can be battling hunger as Christian mission, or they can be serving simply because they are compassionate and caring. Protesters demonstrating as a witness against injustice may or may not be motivated by thankfulness for their own liberation by God's gracious love. We can never be certain that any of our mission activities are totally rooted in God's grace. We can only seek to be faithful to our commitment to engage in the struggle begun by God. We can only be sure that it is God's will that ultimately triumphs.

Giving itself and its substance to the service of those who suffer (G-3.0300c (3), line d)

The fourth dimension of mission is more radical than the third, more challenging to our comfort level. This dimension of mission invites the Presbyterian Church (U.S.A.) to give "itself and its substance." The metaphor of the church as the body of Christ becomes radically evident at this point, where we are corporately invited to commit to service in a total sense. We come to the cross of Christ, there to be willing to serve those who suffer with all that we have and are.

Such a statement appears contrary to the concerns about funding the church's mission. Presbyterians find issues of mission funding intriguing as well as divisive. There never seems to be sufficient funding for all the concerns that the Presbyterian Church (U.S.A.) faces. It has been this way since colonial times, when concern for starting new churches, finding sufficient pastors, and seeking to reach out to Native Americans were already colliding with one another.[17]

Yet line d echoes G-1.0100b: "Christ calls the Church into being, giving it all that is necessary for its mission to the world." In G-3.0102, we are reminded that "in [Christ's] life and death for others God's redeeming love for all people was made visible." To claim to be part of the body of Christ includes trust in the resurrection. Line d crisply challenges us to consider the degree to which we are committed to the key good news we preach.

"How much?" is the continuing stewardship question. The psalmist asked, "What shall I return to the LORD for all his bounty to me?" (Ps. 116:12). How much of what we have and earn do we contribute to the church and its mission? Every fall we respond in some way to the opportunity to pledge or otherwise indicate our intent to support the work of the church. The session and other governing bodies then face the challenge of determining how to use those resources to God's glory.

We have a tendency to consider "our" resources, without remembering that "We give thee but thine own."[18] A major amount of the total budget of our denomination comes from "restricted sources," funds that have been bequeathed for various types of mission. Such funds have come from our predecessor Presbyterians who shared their substance for the purpose of mission. These members of the Church Triumphant enable us to continue serving those who suffer.

Line d presents another ongoing paradox for our life together. Our fellowship has continuing responsibilities that call us to be good stewards of the financial and other resources that are part of our Presbyterian patrimony. At the same time, we must be clear that we are good stewards of what God has given us in order to engage in God's mission shown as to us in Jesus Christ. We will find in the next chapter that we are called to risk.

> Sharing with Christ in the establishing of his just, peaceable, and loving rule in the world. (G-3.0300c (3), line e)

Line e is the final description of what it means to participate "in God's activity in the world." This line echoes the line from the Lord's Prayer, "Thy kingdom come on earth as it is in heaven." This line makes it clear who is doing the establishing: Christ. We are partners in the process, which means that we are serving the LORD, whose kingdom and timetable determine how and when this is done. We find here three adjectives offered as hallmarks of the mission enterprise: just, peaceable, loving.

The Church is called to cooperate with God, to seek God's purpose in God's way as demonstrated in Scripture, and especially in the life, death, and resurrection of Jesus Christ. We are invited to this task, knowing that God will accomplish God's purpose through the Church, whether we Presbyterians, for example, accept the call or not. "Sharing" is yet another of God's gracious acts, offering us opportunity to serve the One we profess as our Lord.

"Just . . . rule in the world." It was noted above that concern for just treatment of widows, orphans, and aliens is a major concern in Deuteronomy. Amos 7:7–9 presents the metaphor of a plumb line amid God's people as a call for justice. Just action is the first of Micah's familiar three requirements of faithfulness to God (Mic. 6:8). Justice was a major concern of the Old Testament prophets, well beyond these two just mentioned.

The key is that it is **God's** just rule that is sought. We frequently hear cries for justice through the media, when relatives of the violated and murdered cry out for "justice." Our Pledge of Allegiance closes with the hope that our country will provide "liberty and justice for all." The wall of separation crumbles at the point of seeking and administering justice.

We Christians realize that the quest for justice at the human level is always a quest, never perfect. People of faith realize that ultimate justice is in God's hands. The plumb line Amos describes is God's ultimate standard of justice. Civil justice is an attempt to maintain order and basic fundamental civility. Sometimes what our country calls for and what the churches seek as an instance of justice coincide – but not always. The Church witnesses to the need for justice across the world, for all people everywhere.

Justice is one of "four major areas of emphasis for the mission work of the Presbyterian Church (U.S.A.) in 2005 and 2006" adopted by the General Assembly Council at its meeting in late September 2003. The justice area is described as follows:

> **Emphasize inclusivity,** in terms of age, gender, orientation, racial-ethnic identity and disability. **Embrace advocacy**—for social witness, economic justice, women's and ethnic concerns, legislative issues, fair housing, health care, environmental protection, etc. **Witness for** peace and non-violence, child

abuse, terrorism and unfair treatment of immigrants and illegal residents.[19]

"Peaceable . . . rule in the world." *Peace* is understood in many different ways. Many define peace as "the absence of trouble." The witness of Scripture differs dramatically from this negative definition. For instance, Isaiah 54 describes the hope of God's coming peace, concluding with the assurance that "I will keep my promise of peace forever" (Isa. 54:10). This is a peace that follows distress and pain, yet is assured of fulfillment by the God whose peace is the ultimate *shalom*.

One of the ironies of the recent past has been the way the major faiths—Christianity, Judaism, and Islam—all include as an item of faith a sense of God's peace. Each has a somewhat different way of pronouncing *shalom*, yet each fervently posits that God is the Giver of peace. It is a quest for wholeness, defined by God. There is a universal yearning in the human heart for peace, for reconciliation, a yearning planted by God.

"Loving rule of the world." The final "sharing with God" is the supreme victory of God's love. This final clause has as much to do with style as with content. Scripture consistently witnesses to God's love, as we have seen in the summary found in G-3.0100. How peculiar it is that churches have such battles over mission strategy when we come to this final clause of G-3.0300! The World Council of Churches recently announced a "Decade to Overcome Violence." Such a call is one way of expressing a response to the invitation to share in God's activity through sharing in the loving rule in the world.

We are brought back by this final clause to Jesus' commandment at the close of the Last Supper:

> Now I give you a new commandment: love one another. As I have loved you, so you must love one another. (John 13:34 TEV)

Content is given in the command to love. Style emerges in the phrase "as I have loved you." That means self-giving, willingness to endure for the sake of the good news.

We have come to the end of the third movement of the mission symphony. We have been reminded that the Church is to tell the good news of salvation, present the claims of Jesus Christ, and to be Christ's faithful evangelist. As one reviews these three major developments, both the essence of mission and the complexity of how mission goes forward have been sketched for us. We may turn to the various representations of what we Presbyterians are to do in mission in our particular churches, presbyteries, and synods, and in the General Assembly Council agencies, and see that we have a comprehensive view of mission as described in this section of our *Book of Order.* How to bring these mission components together continues to be a challenge for us at all levels of church life, for we desire that our mission life together may be a hymn of praise to Jesus Christ.

NOTES

1. *Call* appears 43 times in the Form of Government. The various understandings and uses of the word *call* are discussed in my *History and Theology in the Book of Order* (Louisville: Witherspoon Press, 1999), pp. 35–36.
2. Rev. 2:7, 11, 17, 29; 3:6, 13, 22.
3. *The Book of Confessions,* 4.089.
4. *The Book of Confessions,* 4.090.
5. See *The New Oxford Annotated Bible, New Revised Standard Version,* ed. Bruce M. Metzger and Ronald E. Murphy (New York: Oxford University Press, 1991), "To the reader," xiii.
6. G-3.0200a.
7. *The Book of Confessions,* 6.144.
8. The footnote also refers to Matt. 13:47, 48. A more apt reference would be vs. 40–42, where the weeds are ultimately removed by angels sent by the Son of Man.
9. Luke 9:2.
10. Büchsel, "katallasso" in G. Kittel, ed., *Theological Dictionary of the New Testament,* vol. 1 (Grand Rapids: Wm. B. Eerdmans Publishing Co., 1964), p. 255. Brackets indicate the author's modification from gender-specific to more inclusive pronouns.
11. Ibid., p. 256.
12. Ibid., p. 258.
13. Ibid., p. 255.
14. *The Book of Confessions,* 9.31.
15. "A Brief Statement of Faith" summarizes Jesus' ministry similarly in *The Book of Confessions,* 10.2, lines 9–18.
16. *The Book of Confessions,* 9.12. Other references relating to sin and its pervasiveness are Scots Confession 3.03; Heidelberg Catechism 4.086–091; Second Helvetic Confession 5.037; Westminster Confession 6.031–.036; Shorter Catechism 7.014–.020; Larger Catechism 7.134–140.

17. See Charles Hodge, *A Constitutional History of the Presbyterian Church* (Philadelphia: Presbyterian Board of Publication, 1851; repr. 2000), vol. 2, p. 293, regarding a 1772 "general collection."

18. *The Presbyterian Hymnal* (Louisville: Westminster/John Knox Press, 1990), no. 428.

19. "GAC picks major priorities," by Bill Lancaster. Note #7954 from PCUSA NEWS to PRESBYNEWS (e-mail), September 29, 2003. Emphasis added.

4
FOURTH MOVEMENT: CHALLENGED

Sprung Time (G-3.0400)

The opening phrase of the fourth movement repeats the refrain of previous movements, "The Church is called." G-3.0400 is followed by four subparagraphs, all beginning with the phrase "to a new openness. . . . " This repetition hammers home a challenge to us as we stand on the threshold of the future of mission.

Were this movement to be set to music, I would suggest what is called "sprung time," 5/4 time. A movement of Tchaikovsky's *Symphonie Pathétique* is perhaps the most accessible illustration of sprung time in classical music. In the late twentieth century, a jazz piece called "Unsquare Dance" by David Brubeck became popular in spite of its odd time or meter. Brubeck's oratorio on the life of Jesus, *Light in the Wilderness,* also uses the 5/4 meter to emphasize those times in Jesus' life when he faced difficult decisions, such as the temptations (Matt. 4:1–11).[1] An even more challenging analogy would be the "Indian ragas" as interpreted by Philip Glass and described as "droning, trancelike . . . , which evolve over hours-long or all-night performances into seemingly simple (but, in fact immensely complex) dialogues of themes and rhythms."[2]

Choosing a meter that is deliberately offbeat alerts us to the challenges of this final movement of the mission symphony. We will find ourselves challenged by the text as we are tested by the difficulties we encounter in living the Christian life. This provision of the *Book of Order* alerts us that we need to move beyond what we consider our comfort zone. We will be invited to "think outside the box," which is what has been said by those impatient with what they consider the strictures of the *Book of Order.*

One might well say that this section (G-3.0400) is perhaps the most radical in the *Book of Order.* These five short paragraphs build on and extend the motto of the Reformed movement in G-2.0200, " 'The church reformed, always reforming,' according to the Word of God and the call of the Spirit." The basis for this motto comes from such biblical sources as Isaiah 24:19–20 (and Isa. 6:4), Jesus' teaching about new wine in old wineskins,[3] and Paul's reminder in 2 Corinthians 4:7 that "we have this treasure in clay pots." That this section of our *Book of Order* has escaped the attention of Presbyterians, as we have struggled with currents of change in church policies, strikes one as curious.

This view subordinates our role to that of God, who is at work among us and through us. "Reforming" differs from revolution, understood as radical change during a brief time. We are called to listen, to "open the windows" as Pope John XXIII famously put it.

To be open requires humility. Often the key to improvement lies in careful listening to those with whom we disagree. Many seem always in a hurry for everything, from the simplest chores of life to weightier matters. Being in a hurry leads us to interrupt others in conversation, to cut off others in traffic. The sad paradox is that in spite of our desire to "save time" with new, improved gadgets, there still never seems to be enough time.

To be open requires trust in God. To be open is to dream, to consider possibilities, to explore new understandings. Hope differs from desire in that it is open-ended, daring to risk what is new, willing to find dead ends and then channel our efforts in a more fruitful direction. To be open is to be prepared to grow.

We find these challenges in the opening sentence, a rousing call in the main clause that rings out as a trumpet call:[4]

"The Church is called to undertake this mission even at the risk of losing its life."

Such a comment strikes us as an extreme measure, like a pail of cold water thrown on a sleeper in order to wake the person up. "This mission" connects what follows from the delineation of the scope of mission in G-3.0300.

The so-called Age of Affluence[5] in the United States has lulled us into a sense of comfort with the way things are. We tend to shy away from comments or deeds that seem to rock the boat. The sudden decline in the stock market in the early years of the twenty-first century devastated many when the darker side of life reemerged. When this was followed by the terrorist attack of September 11, 2001, many found themselves traumatized by still another evidence that comfort was not an abiding aspect of life.

Scripture gives us numerous illustrations of the importance of sacrifice. One instance is in Hebrews 9:12, where we are given a comparison of the high priest in the Holy of Holies with Jesus Christ: "He entered once for all into the Holy Place, not with the blood of goats and calves, but with his own blood, thus obtaining eternal redemption."

A more subtle yet compelling phrase is Jesus' new commandment in John 15:12: "This is my commandment, that you love one another as I have loved you." We tend to consider Jesus' commandment from the viewpoint of the quality or feeling of "love" as we understand it. The next sentence clarifies Jesus' intent: "No one has greater love than this, to lay down one's life for one's friends." There is indeed a cross at the center of our faith. Resurrection assures us that death is not God's final word, while enabling us to "give up" in obedience to our Lord.

This clause echoes a phrase found in the "Confession of 1967," where a discussion of the relevance of reconciliation for "peace, justice, and freedom among nations" calls upon Presbyterians to "pursue fresh and responsible relations across every line of conflict, **even at risk to national security.**"[6] During the period when the United Presbyterian Church in the United States of America was debating whether to adopt this confession and the *Book of Confessions*, this phrase became a lightning rod for the dispute.

The expression in G-4.0000 strikes us as a major conundrum. To think that "mission" risks the existence of a church! What could the drafters have been thinking of? The answer is, simply, Jesus as the model for mission, the Jesus who was willing to be crucified.

Scripture also witnesses to the disciples' need to give of themselves, trusting and risking simultaneously. Matthew's account of the feeding of the five thousand shows that the five loaves and two fish the disciples have is sufficient to feed the multitude and have twelve baskets left over.[7] The apostle Paul wrote to the Ephesians that God "is able to accomplish abundantly far more than all we can ask or imagine" (Eph. 3:20).[8] We now are challenged to accept that the Church as the body of Christ may in fact be called to go to the cross, just as the Lord of the Church went to the cross.

Our obligation to "go into all the world" is also a challenge. After several years of struggling with the challenges of mission, the Synod of New York and Philadelphia, on May 25, 1767, adopted an "introduction" for their "Collection for Pious Purposes" that demonstrates both the depth and the scope of their concern:

> The Synod laying to Heart the unhappy Lot of many People, in Various Parts of our Land, who, at present are brought up in Ignorance; and that they & their Families are perishing for lack of Knowledge, who, on Account of their Poverty, or Scattered Habitations are unable without some Assistance to Support the Gospel ministry among them; Considering also, that it is their Duty to send Missionaries to the frontier Settlements, who may Preach to the dispersed Families, there, and form them into Societies, for the public Worship of God, and being moved with Compassion toward the Indians, especially those under our Care, who are extremely Poor, & Unable to teach their Children to Read, or to Instruct them in the Knowledge of the Holy Scriptures, have resolved to Attempt their relief, and to Instruct such as may be willing to hear the Gospel.[9]

This was how our forebears prefaced the announcement of an offering for mission. What is interesting is how broad the concern was: it included building churches, education for all, and evangelism among Native Americans. It also reveals deep concern for mission and for people.

Most of us recognize that the first words the angels said to frightened shepherds were, "Fear not" (Luke 2:10 KJV). A concordance lists 24 times in the Old Testament when God or one of God's chosen uses this expression in exhorting the faithful to courage.[10] The most poignant instance for me is in Deuteronomy 31:8, when Moses commissions Joshua to be his successor. The commission to Joshua is one we need to hear and remember as we consider the implications of the challenge to openness. I find Everett Fox's translation especially helpful in conveying the power of the Hebrew text:

> And YHWH, he is the one who goes before you,
> he will be with you;
> he will not fail you, he will not abandon you;
> you are not to be overawed, you are not to be shattered![11]

The Church is called to undertake this mission even at the risk of losing its life, **trusting in God alone as the author and giver of life** . . .

This next phrase provides the theological basis for what strikes us initially as outrageous. The theme of trust provides the framework of "A Brief Confession of Faith."[12] The commentary on this confession cites Psalm 115, verses 4–9, then proceeds:

> There you have it, the connection between where we put our trust and what sort of persons or things we become. Knowing that we belong to the living God entails certain realities which are to be reconfessed, in word and action. Such active, critical reconfession is continually refocused as believers are moved to trust and obey, in life and in death, the one Word who is Jesus Christ as he is attested to in the scriptures.[13]

The authors remind us of the significance of the Second Commandment's prohibition against reverencing anything other than God the Lord.

We are tempted in many ways to rely on the Church we know as the means of our support and salvation. Such a temptation is subtle and persuasive, yet inimical to vital faith in Jesus Christ as Lord and Savior. We are saved and empowered by God's grace in Jesus Christ alone. We are grateful to the Church for telling and reminding us that Jesus Christ brings good news to us. At the same time, we must be aware that the church we love is a vessel, not the substance, of our faith. We trust God alone!

The God we trust is "the author and giver of life." This brief phrase names God as the Author of life itself, the Source of all sentient being. The life I have is a gift from God, and so is the life of all my brothers and sisters on the planet now and forever. "Author" gives a nuance that "Creator" has come to lack. There is freshness to the expression, recognizing God's creativity in providing for life.

God gives life to you and me. The Author does not withhold life, but gives it generously. Many of us take life for granted, as if we (or our parents) somehow invented the process. We cherish "our" life, keep it for ourselves, protect "our" lives. Life is precious to us. But life doesn't belong to us. It is a gift from God, who asks that we live grateful lives, giving what we are to one another.

This discussion derives from the Presbyterian understanding of the importance of God's sovereignty. We learn to trust from our mothers. We eventually also learn how complicated it is to determine whom and what we can trust. We may be surprised at the radical implication of how seriously we are to take God's sovereignty, especially its significance for determining whom we can trust. It is a reminder we need to heed.

This statement invites us to stand with Moses at the burning bush (Ex. 3), hearing the call from our holy God, trembling and kneeling, and then discovering that we must be obedient to the heavenly vision (Isa. 6; Acts 26:19). As one rises from such an encounter, John affirms, "perfect love casts out fear" (1 John 4:18).

> The Church is called to undertake this mission even at the risk of losing its life, trusting in God alone as the author and giver of life, **sharing the gospel.** . . .

It is only when trust in God's redeeming and forgiving love has begun to transform us that we are able to begin **sharing the gospel.** Were we to attempt to convince others of God's mercy and love without ourselves knowing it, we would be attempting the impossible. We would find our effort to be frustratingly ineffective.

The gospel is for sharing. D. T. Niles, the ecumenical statesman from the Church of South India, taught the Western churches this truth: "Evangelism is one beggar telling another beggar where to find bread." We in the affluent West may find this difficult to imagine. But it reminds us that while we were yet sinners, Christ died for us. Mission is indeed impossible without primary trust in Jesus Christ as Lord.

This phrase ties in with the earlier discussion of mission as telling the good news, being Christ's faithful evangelist (G-3.0300). What is added is the dimension of trust as a critical component for such enterprises.

> The Church is called to undertake this mission even at the risk of losing its life, trusting in God alone as the author and giver of life, sharing the gospel, **and doing those deeds in the world that point beyond themselves to the new reality in Christ.**

Trusting faith is even more essential when we begin **doing those deeds that point beyond themselves.** So often we hear the lament of the faithful, "What's the use?" Contemporary American Christians have given in to the prevalent passion of getting immediate results, whatever the enterprise. Persistence is often seen as stubbornness or evidence of unreality. Some Presbyterian preacher years ago preached about "keeping on keeping on." That became a motto in our family as we went about seeking to be faithful. It sums up the third and final phrase of the introductory clause.

This phrase restates G-3.0300c(3). The focus is on working out the practical implications of praying, "Thy kingdom come." Presbyterians tend not to spend much time considering the "last things" as an aspect of theology. We are aware that there is more to life than the here and now. We can't say the Lord's Prayer without some recognition that God will resolve what sometimes appears little more than chaos. The hope we have in Christ (G-1.0100d) is meaningless unless there comes a time when God's rule is victorious. You and I can only point in that direction, but point we must, to be faithful. Such action pointing forward cannot happen without relying confidently on the promise of our Lord.

As we come to the end of chapter III, we find four specifications as to the nature of the risk identified in G-3.0400. The one-line expression in G-3.0401, "The Church is called," continues the form followed in G-3.0300. There follow four specifications, each of which is introduced by the words "to a new openness." It is only when we are prepared to trust God alone that we are able to open ourselves. What is startling is finding such radical material in the *Book of Order.*

The first type of openness repeats the complex form we have seen throughout this chapter.

> The Church is called
> to a new openness to the presence of God in the Church
> and in the world,
> to more fundamental obedience, and
> to a more joyous celebration in worship and work. . . .

The first openness is both spiritual and theological. In G-3.0103, there was an affirmation that God through the Holy Spirit calls humans to repentance and obedience. Since that reference, time and again we find the refrain "God calls the Church." It is easy to forget that there must be some readiness to listen. Ever since Moses encountered God at the burning bush (Ex. 3), persons have been astonished by their call to serve the Lord God. The prophets of the Old Testament, as well as those called by Jesus to be disciples, recover from their amazement, then respond to serve God obediently.

The alert is sounded, that we are called to "new openness to the presence of God." While there is a New Age sound to this material, adopted in 1983, there are clear echoes of Bible for us, beginning with our understanding of God as Creator (G-3.0101a). Isaiah might properly be called the prophet of the new, since he preached that God said, "I am about to do a new thing" (Isa. 43:19), after warning against remembering the former things (v. 18). In Isaiah 65:17, Isaiah reports God's message as, "For I am about to create new heavens and a new earth; the former things shall not be remembered." This latter proclamation inspired a later prophet in the book of Revelation (21:1) to exclaim, "Then I saw a new heaven and a new earth; for the first heaven and the first earth had passed away." The dilemma we face is portrayed in Jesus' words to his disciples in Matthew 13:52: "Every scribe who has been trained for the kingdom of heaven is like the master of a household who brings out of his treasure what is new and what is old."

"Presence of God" does not stand alone. To the phrase is added, **"in the Church and in the world. . . . "** God's sovereignty means that God is always present in creation, which includes the whole world of perception and experience. "Openness" suggests a willingness to listen, to learn, to expand our awareness. We find ourselves wrestling with the tension between what we know and hold dear on the one hand, and those unfamiliar, strange, unexpected ideas and experiences that surround us. We seem caught between the dead hand of tradition ("we never did it that way before," also known as the seven last words of a church) and the siren song of possibilities.

> The Church is called . . .
> to more fundamental obedience. . . .

"New openness to God," according to the text, leads "to more fundamental obedience." This suggests to me that we have here a modern way of referring to sanctification, which the Westminster Shorter Catechism defines as a process whereby, through God's grace, we "are enabled more and more to die unto sin and live unto righteousness."[14] With Paul, we learn to say, "Forgetting what lies behind and straining forward to what lies ahead, I press on toward the goal for the prize of the heavenly call of God in Christ Jesus."[15] There is also an echo of Acts 26:19, where Paul, after telling Agrippa of the Damascus road experience, continued, "I was not disobedient to the heavenly vision," continuing to summarize what he had done.

"More fundamental obedience" is both deepened faith and energized witness. How one determines what is to be done, to God's glory, within the fellowship of the church differs from person to person. The obedience is to the God who speaks to us in a way that cannot be resisted, even if we are periodically uncomfortable with what we hear. "Reformed and reforming" has as much to do with each of us as we grow in discipleship as it does for the church as a community.

The Church is called . . .
to a more joyous celebration in worship and work. . . .

There is another sort of surprise that comes as we discover the word *joyous* as the final component of the first openness. *Joy* in its various forms is not a word commonly associated with Presbyterians, or with the *Book of Order*. Yet we find it here, another surprise as we venture into openness. There are 39 occurrences of *joy* and its cognates on the CD version of the *Book of Order,* 7 occurrences in the Form of Government, 9 in the Directory for Worship.

The church is called to "more joyous celebration **in worship and work.**" Joy is not a synonym for fun. Joy is profound, arising from deep within us, a quality that suffuses our whole being, leaving a sense of well-being, while "fun" is amusement, distraction, a fleeting thing. Joy can be solemn, as what floods over us when baptism or Communion is celebrated. Worship is where we learn with others that there is such a thing as holy joy. Joy is a gift that comes with worship, one that cannot be engineered but is there to be received when one is open and receptive.

If we seldom experience joy in worship, if we believe that joy is not something we should expect in worship, we are even less likely to associate joy with work. Much work is drudgery, especially if it is doing the same thing over and over. Two summers working shifts on an automotive line where the next unit arrived every two minutes and forty seconds taught me how mind-numbing such labor could be. I was glad to get back to college when summer was over.

Work as an aspect of openness might affect mission in two ways. The first would be to equip workers with resources to deal with the deadening sameness of their work. William McKay became the pastor of the North Presbyterian Church in Lansing, Michigan, in the 1930s, when unemployment in factories was at its height. McKay had worked for the YMCA, so when he discovered that North Church had a gymnasium, he organized an exercise program for those out of work. He understood that if they were not working, they would become less and less able to work. Understandably, when men from the program were hired, they kept their jobs longer than those who had been idle.

The other prong of mission related to work is seeking remedies for practices that dehumanize and/or denigrate persons responsible for producing the necessities of our society. This approach to mission is slower to "show results," yet offers possibilities when sustained and led with patience and courage. Such so-called activist approaches seeking amelioration of harsh working environments and other dehumanizing conditions have from time to time produced identifiable social changes in ways that are much less likely to emerge in the world of secular political governance.

The church gathers persons with diverse gifts for service and ministry. No one mission strategy will appeal to everyone. The point we sometimes overlook is that we need one another, we need mission going forward in multiple directions, all obedient to the Lord of the Church.

The second "openness" to which the church is called, according to G-3.0401b, is openness

> " . . . to its own membership,
> by affirming itself as a community of diversity,
> becoming in fact as well as in faith
> a community of women and men of all ages,
>   races, and conditions,
> and by providing for inclusiveness as a visible
>   sign of the new humanity."

This provision in chapter III reflects the situation of the historic reunion of 1983, between the United Presbyterian Church in the United States of America and the Presbyterian Church in the United States after 121 years of separation. Other evidences of reunion can be found in G-4.0400, "Diversity and Inclusiveness"; G-9.0104–.0106 regarding representation; Articles 7 and 8 of the "Articles of Agreement" ("Special Committee on Presbytery and Synod Boundaries" and "Racial Ethnic Representation, Participation and Organizations"). Article 8, which continues to appear in Appendix B of the *Book of Order*, tells clearly what the concerns were: "All governing bodies shall work to become more open and inclusive and to correct past patterns of discrimination on the basis of racial ethnic background."[16] The 208th General Assembly (1996) adopted the goal of increasing the racial ethnic membership to 10 percent of the total membership by 2005, and to 20 percent by 2010.[17] A strategy for fulfilling these goals, including funding, and requiring annual reports of progress, was adopted by the 210th General Assembly (1998).[18]

The increasing immigration of Presbyterians from other countries who seek fellowship with us has opened new opportunities for us to respond to the second call for openness. The adoption in 1999 of a new provision (G-11.0404f) enabling presbyteries to recognize the ordination of immigrant pastors "if it determines that its strategy for mission with that constituency requires it" is another evidence of seeking to fulfill the openness called for.

The degree to which our reunited Presbyterian Church and its members have succeeded in the vision of "new openness" is still open to question. Openness to the diversity in the Presbyterian family is still a call, and it still requires energy and sensitivity. Some progress emerges here and there, yet enormous differences remain to be overcome.

The vision here is not sociological or psychological or political; it is deeply theological. The reason for this is Scripture's consistent witness to God's openness in seeking those who respond to God's call. Tension is evident as we ponder this second call, when we realize that we are the ones called to be open. Each of us determines how open we will be to brothers and sisters who differ from us. As a church, we also determine how open we will be to those who differ from us. These are never easy decisions, as we have learned in the struggle since 1976 regarding what are now called alternate lifestyles. What seems to be lost in the disputes that have been the focus of much of our corporate lives as Presbyterians is that your and my decisions about who is in or out are always measured by the One who is the ultimate Judge of us all.

A deeper issue that is engendering controversy is the call to the church to become open " . . . by affirming itself as a community of diversity." Since reunion, and possibly because of it, the call to affirm the Presbyterian Church (U.S.A.) as a "community of diversity" has been a focal concern for nearly thirty years. Enormous amounts of time, money, and energy have been poured into this dispute. Presbyterian sociologist William Weston suggests that both extremes in the church have fostered the myth of conflict between the "right" and "left" wings of the church, while historically and sociologically, the dispute has been a struggle for the support of the moderate loyalist center, the pillars of the church, who are "the defenders of constitutional practices, and mollifiers of all constituencies."[19] Weston points out that Presbyterians have had these disputes in the past, and have been resolved in various ways. At this point, it is still unclear how this latest controversy will be resolved, and at what additional cost.

The third openness "challenge" is laid out for us in G-3.0401c:

> to a new openness to the possibilities and perils
> of its institutional forms
> in order to ensure the faithfulness and
> usefulness of these forms
> to God's activity in the world.

Some might say that this "openness" is one about which Presbyterians need not worry. They would point to the restructures that seemed to characterize the last half of the twentieth century. Restructure, realignment, and reunion were major activities at the various levels of our fellowship. "Usefulness" has tended to be the major criterion for these structural rearrangements.

People of faith tend to be optimists, at least in the long run. Optimists are more likely to see the possibilities in institutional forms, while pessimists (or realists) discern the perils. Both views have a measure of truth. The important distinction from the Westminster Confession between the purity of the invisible church and the mixture of the visible church testifies to this ambiguity.

It is currently popular to call for "thinking outside the box." This phrase suggests a yearning for something better, something fresh, something new and invigorating to come into our lives. At the same time, there is another tension, a fear that change will bring "unanticipated consequences," which will become even more challenging than those with which we currently contend.

You and I are created with bodies, which we use in various ways yet cannot escape, at least not for long. We imagine and dream, then return to who and where we are, to how God made us. We learn or are reminded that we are finite, that we have limits. We test the limits, discover which are the ones beyond which we cannot go. We learn eventually, and sometimes painfully, that promises that seem too good to be true generally are.

As people of faith, we recognize another set of tensions. We seek to be faithful disciples following Jesus Christ, the Word made flesh. We recognize that the Reformed tradition includes openness to change "according to the Word of God and the call of the Spirit."[20] We learn that the box we seek to escape is composed of unexamined traditions that arise so easily and resist review in the light of our "standards."

Paul's metaphor for the church as the body of Christ lies behind G-3.0401c. The phrase, "the faithfulness and usefulness of these forms to God's activity in the world," restates 1 Corinthians 12:12–27 in contemporary language. These are the criteria for a church polity as well as for the particular parts of the church. These criteria indicate that there may well be times when a particular aspect of church life no longer fulfills these requirements. When such an evaluation is reached, it is time to review, reconstruct, or at least surgically remove the no longer productive entity. These two criteria indicate both a theological and a missiological concern. "Faithful" and "useful" seem to point in different directions, yet here they are combined to remind us that structures have to meet both tests.

The debate on the role of synods since 1969 has tended in this direction. Although Overture 55 in 1996 from the Presbytery of the James calling for a "study as to whether the governing layer of synod continues to be a necessary and effective part of our church structure"[21] was disapproved by the 208th General Assembly, synods have since then have made major changes in structure and operation. Subsequently, mission effectiveness has increased in many instances.

Beyond the two criteria discussed, the ultimate criterion is "God's activity in the world." What we do in mission is always "follow the Leader." Discerning what God is doing in the world is a much more daunting task than restructure. There are no outside organizational consultants we can bring in for this activity. Mission suggests that our question needs to be, "What is God up to now?" The Old and New Testaments, especially as summarized in G-3.0101–0102 suggest that God has consistently demonstrated surprising creativity amid the speculations and convictions of those who sought to follow God's ways.

The fourth and final openness (G-3.0401d) is:

> to God's continuing reformation of the Church ecumenical, that it might be a more effective instrument of mission in the world.

John A. Mackay, when president of Princeton Theological Seminary, often told his students about the evening in the late 1930s at the president's home on campus when Archbishop William Temple first used the word *ecumenical* to describe what was emerging as "world-wide

Christianity."[22] Dr. Mackay would proceed to explain how the word was taken from the Greek (*oikumenē*), meaning "the inhabited earth." Presbyterians had already been engaged in the International Missionary Conference, beginning in Edinburgh in 1910.[23]

Cooperative mission had been rooted in our tradition before then. The Plan of Union between Congregationalists and Presbyterians began in 1801 as a strategy for planting churches on the frontier. This cooperative enterprise would subsequently become a factor in the division of 1837–38 into Old School and New School.[24]

The roots of cooperation lie much deeper in our Presbyterian heritage. In her seminal volume, Janet Macgregor concludes: "So far as may be judged from the internal evidence to be gathered from a comparative study of the polity of the Scottish Church of 1560, that Church appears to be highly composite in origin."[25] Macgregor demonstrates that John Knox was influenced by his extensive contacts with Reformed colleagues and their various understandings of how to organize the life of churches. Macgregor closes with the following comment relevant to our discussion:

> Varied as were the foreign sources from which the Scottish reformers drew, in building up their sixteenth-century polity, one great debt modern Presbyterianism owes to the Scottish Church itself. It was in Scotland that the opportunity first occurred for testing Presbyterian institutions by applying them in the government of a national Church.[26]

In *The Second Book of Discipline* adopted by the General Assembly in 1578, the following is especially pertinent to our understanding of ecumenical roots:

> Assemblies are of four sorts. For either are they of particular kirks and congregations one or more, or of a province, or of one whole nation, or of all and divers nations professing one Jesus Christ.[27]

The last kind of assembly is described as follows:

> There is besides these, another more general kind of assembly, which is of all nations and estates of persons within the kirk, representing the universal kirk of Christ: Which may be called properly the General Assembly or General Council of the whole kirk of God.
>
> These assemblies were appointed and called together, especially when any great schism or controversy of doctrine did arise

in the kirk, and were convoked at command of godly emperors being for the time, for avoiding schisms within the universal kirk of God: Which because they appertain not to the particular estate of one realm, we cease further to speak of them.[28]

This fourth level of assembly is that represented by the ecumenical councils of history, such as Nicaea and Constantinople. That the Assembly included mention of these in their polity indicates the breadth of their vision.

As evidence that we Presbyterians have understood G-3.0401d, there is chapter XV, "Relationships." The opening paragraph (G-15.0101) bears the title "Openness," where we pledge to "be open to opportunities for conversation, cooperation, and action with other ecclesiastical bodies and secular groups." The remainder of the chapter develops some implications of this openness.

We also have "A Formula of Agreement" with three other denominations, approved in 1997–98, which is included as appendix C in our *Book of Order*. The breakthrough concept in these discussions was "the complementarity of mutual affirmation and mutual admonition."[29] There is also a "Statement of Ecumenical Consensus," approved in 1999 and 2000, called "Visible Marks of Churches Uniting in Christ."[30]

These are some of the specific ways we Presbyterians continue to seek to be "a more effective instrument of mission in the world." Our predecessors have set us on this road, this tradition of understanding that we have much to share with others who claim Jesus Christ as Lord. One expression of this tradition came from a General Assembly commission's response to a request from Los Angeles Presbytery in 1953 for a ruling regarding ministers engaging in non-Presbyterian-related ministries:

> This has meant that in America we have had the development, unparalleled elsewhere in the world, of inter-denominational and non-denominational Christian activity. From the very beginnings of our Church we as Presbyterians have been the organizers, the leaders, the educators; the supporters, and the members of countless numbers of these inter-denominational and non-denominational ventures. Only rarely, and never for any one long period of time, has the Presbyterian Church in the United States of America shown any desire to be a narrow "ism": Rather, it has been one of the foremost among the American Churches in its longing to be a vital part of the total Christian life and work within our nation. The cost, however,

of maintaining this attitude has been serious for our Church during most of its history.[31]

This dispute arose from mission concerns and led to the inclusion of G-11.0410–.0411.

Postlude

We Presbyterians have historically asked, in one way or another, "How open should we be?" These four challenges to openness suggest that the deeper issue is, "To whom must we be open?" Faithfulness becomes openness to God's leading, trusting deeply in God's gracious purpose for those who seek to serve God. Mission such as this is impossible without the conviction that Jesus Christ is the hope of the Church. Without such hope and trust, mission is impossible. So is the freedom "to live in the lively, joyous reality of the grace of God" (G-1.0100d).

Each of us should focus on using the gifts God has given us in mission to God's greater glory. Where we get into disputes is when we judge the mission our brother or sister has chosen to serve as encroaching on what we ourselves are doing. Examined from this perspective, the wrangling about specific forms of denominational mission suggests two problems of our life together. The first is the notion that offerings to Christ's mission are best understood the way we currently understand our taxes to government: that there is somehow a string attached to whatever we give, allowing us to pull back when someone takes "our money" and some portion goes toward some project or activity to which we object. It seems to me that this is contrary to Jesus' teaching about money in Matthew 22:15–22, and that such a position reveals that our offering is given to the church, rather than to God.

The second problem, I suggest, is a loss of focus on whose mission we are called to undertake. The mission I really think is important may not be the same as what the person sitting next to me in the pew on Sunday would choose. When we make decisions on the validity of someone else's sense of mission, we need to bear in mind Jesus' comment about judging: "With the judgment you make you will be judged" (Matt. 7:2). God alone is the ultimate judge of all of our decisions. As some folks say, "We all have a lot to be humble about."

The tension between conviction and openness is at the heart of our life together as Presbyterians. Reviewing our history suggests how pervasive this paradox has been for us in all periods. Often there have been painful, bitter battles between Presbyterians with strongly held yet differing convictions. Through it all, the Presbyterian Church has survived. Mission has gone forward, sometimes stumbling, sometimes with such vigor that we are still astounded at what we have accomplished. It is then that we realize that all of us are graced to serve the Lord of all, who is able to take even our disputes and move ever onward to achieve the purpose that we yearn for—together with our faithful predecessors and all those who will follow us—the coming of God's kingdom in God's good time.

NOTES

1. Writing about Gesualdo di Venosa (1561–1613), James Keller says, "[Gesualdo's] music is 'dissonant' in a profound sense, jarring in melody, harmony, and rhythm. This is not to suggest that his works are in any sense 'unmusical,' for they are not. But they certainly did stretch the boundaries of composition, even at a time when boundaries were generally stretched, and the avant-garde character of his madrigals has not faded with the passage of centuries." "Notes for 'Monumentum' pro Gesualda di Venosa ad CD Annum, by Igor Stravinsky," in *Playbill*, New York Philharmonic, November 2003, p. 29.
2. Harry Sumrall, "Master Glass," in *Smithsonian* 34, no. 8 (November 2003): 104.
3. Matt. 9:17; Mark 2:22; Luke 5:37–38.
4. I wish to acknowledge that the inspiration for the tone of this section came from a sermon, "If We Confess Our Sins . . ." preached by Rev. J. Michael Pulsifer, pastor of the Ridgewood, New Jersey, West Side Presbyterian Church, November 9, 2003.
5. The phrase "Age of Affluence" reveals a preoccupation with economics as the only meaningful perspective on our world. "So-called" is added to remind us that Christian faith is more comprehensive, more realistic perspective.
6. *The Book of Confessions*, 9.45. Perhaps the most intense discussion was on the floor of what was called the Washington City Presbytery, where Rev. George M. Docherty and Rev. Edward L. R. Elson engaged in a spirited debate regarding this clause.
7. Matthew 14:13–21.
8. I heard the pairing of these lessons (Matt. 14:13–21 and Eph. 3:20) at the West Side Presbyterian Church in Ridgewood, New Jersey, on Sunday, October 12, 2003, in the sermon by Rev. J. Michael Pulsifer.
9. Guy S. Klett, ed., *Minutes of the Presbyterian Church in America 1706–1788* (Philadelphia: Presbyterian Historical Society, 1976), pp. 433–34. Spelling has been modernized.

10. "Fear not": Gen. 15:1; 21:17; 26:24; 35:17; 43:23; 50:19, 21; Ex. 14:13; 20:20; Num. 14:9; 21:34; Deut. 1:21; 3:2, 22; 20:3; 31:6, 8; Josh. 8:1; 10:8, 24; Judg. 4:18; 6:10, 23; 1 Sam. 4:20; 22:23; 2 Sam. 9:7; 13:28; 1 Kings 17:13; 2 Kings 6:16; 17:38; 1 Chron. 28:20.

11. Everett Fox, *The Five Books of Moses,* vol. 1 of *The Schocken Bible* (New York: Schocken Books, 1983), p. 997.

12. "A Brief Statement of Faith," *Book of Confessions,* lines 5, 27, 52.

13. William C. Placher and David Willis-Watkins, *Belonging to God: A Commentary on A Brief Statement of Faith* (Louisville: Westminster/John Knox Press, 1992), p. 48.

14. *The Book of Confessions,* 7.035.

15. Phil. 3:13b–14.

16. *Book of Order,* appendix B, pp. B-8–B-9.

17. *Minutes of the 208th General Assembly (1996),* vol. I, p. 378, para. 33.148.

18. *Minutes of the 210th General Assembly (1998),* vol. I, p. 415, para. 22.0545–0550A.

19. William J. Weston, *Leading from the Center: Strengthening the Pillars of the Church* (Louisville: Geneva Press, 2003), p. 2.

20. G-2.0200.

21. *Minutes of the 208th General Assembly* (1996), Part I, *Journal,* 715.

22. Personal recollection from a lecture in Dr. Mackay's class in ecumenics.

23. See Theodore A. Gill, Jr., "American Presbyterians in the Global Ecumenical Movement," in Coalter, Mulder, and Weeks, eds., *The Diversity of Discipleship* (Louisville: Westminster/John Knox Press, 1991), p. 130ff.

24. James H. Smylie, *A Brief History of the Presbyterians* (Louisville: Geneva Press, 1996), p. 72.

25. Janet G. Macgregor, *The Scottish Presbyterian Polity: A Study of Its Origins in the Sixteenth Century* (Edinburgh: Oliver & Boyd, 1926), p. 61.

26. Ibid., p. 136.

27. *The Second Buik of Discipline or Heidis and Conclusiones of the Policie of the Kirk agreed upon in the General Assembly, 1578* (Sterotyped by L. Johnson & Co., Philadelphia, n.d.), chap. VII:2, p. xxx. The passage has been rendered in modern English from the text by the author.

28. Ibid., pp. xxxiv–xxxv, chap. VII:40 and 41.

29. *Book of Order,* appendix C, p. C-3.

30. *Book of Order,* appendix D.

31. *From the Annotated Book of Order,* 2002–2003, CD version, under the title "G-11.0406 (2), PCUSA, 1953, pp. 110–133. Presbytery of Los Angeles Memorial & Ovt J."

A FINAL REFLECTION

After listening to a symphony, a music lover ponders how the piece developed, what it was that held the music together. Similarly, this "mission symphony" offers a progressive theological discussion seldom found elsewhere. Now that you have walked with me through these reflections, one more reflection could produce a deeper and broader understanding of our mission as Presbyterians.

The beginning of mission, according to "The Church and Its Mission," is recalling what God has done as shown in the Bible. Presbyterian mission begins at creation, rather than at the end of Matthew's Gospel. Mission is involvement with what God had intended all along. You and I are invited to work alongside the Creator! God's purpose is laid out in G-3.0100 so that we can appreciate how we go about fulfilling God's intent. The Trinity is the ultimate resource for mission.

God has always invited humans to be coworkers. Scripture tells how those invited to be God's people have responded. As God's people were in the past, the Church is a fellowship called to be obedient, to respond to God's call, to accept God's leading. The definitions of Church in G-3.0200 are both inviting and daunting, a human attempt to work out what it means to be about God's business. These definitions add layers of meaning to what we usually mean when we speak about church. The implication is that to be church is to be about God's mission.

What then, are we to do? G-3.0300 provides a bridge between two previous sections with a contemporary interpretation of how we understand God's intent as shown in the Bible. There is a comprehensive mission outlined in this section. In the ongoing disputes about what constitutes mission, these lines provide a template that continues to fit with what we Presbyterians do at the various levels of the Church. None of us have all the gifts or understanding to do all these. God has blessed us with diverse gifts that enable us to work together, faithfully responding to God's call to God's people.

The mission symphony ends with mission challenges (G-3.0400). Lest we unduly glorify mission, the symphony ends with a reminder of risks in mission, when we enter Calvary's shadow, which falls over every Christian. We hear four calls to a "new openness." We face choices that lead us beyond the familiar and the comfortable. God calls us to faithfulness, to "celebrate the journey now and praise the Lord."[1]

NOTES

1. From "Come Sing, O Church, in Joy," by Brian Dill, *The Presbyterian Hymnal* (Louisville: Westminster/John Knox Press, 1990), no. 430.

LEADER'S GUIDE

~

Initial considerations. This book uses a musical metaphor as a structural device. I propose that preparing to use this guide as background to the study will contribute to the success of your process. The guide leads to the suggestion that you plan to use CDs or other audio as a way of preparing the environment and the participants for their experience. Another possibility would be to plan to sing a hymn together at the beginning or end of each session.

At the end of this guide, there is a listing of resources for additional study. Depending on the nature of your group and your own level of interest in mission, these resources offer background potentially useful as you lead the group through a careful consideration of G-3.0000. An optimal number of sessions is six, as follows:

1. Introductory: the basic text (G-3.0100)
2. God's activity and mission (G-3.0100-.0103)
3. Church and mission (G-3.0200)
4. The Church's calling to mission (G-3.0300)
5. Mission and risk (G-3.0400)
6. What are we going to do?

Detailed suggestions for each session follow.

I. Introductory Session

A. As participants arrive,
   1. Have Beethoven's Fifth Symphony playing softly in the background.
   2. Display the world mission map from the Program Calendar.
   3. Distribute copies of the book to the participants.

    4. Greet participants as they arrive, get names, and distribute or sell books.

B. Explain why Beethoven's Fifth Symphony was playing as they entered. The title of the book, *Mission Symphony,* uses "symphony" as a metaphor for the material to be covered.

    1. Replay the opening bars of Beethoven's Fifth.

    2. Discuss how these four notes are the foundation for the entire symphony, developed, reworked, inverted, and so forth.

    3. Begin to explore the themes used in the discussion of mission in chapter III of our *Book of Order*'s Form of Government.

C. Explain that the people in the group come with some understanding of "mission." Invite each person to share what she or he understands by the word *mission.* Write down the various understandings and comments on newsprint without comment. [Keep these initial comments for use in the final session.]

D. Invite questions about mission from the group members. [Write these on newsprint or some other form, so that responses to these may be elicited during the study.]

E. Present G-3.0100 to the class. [This might be on a card, written on a board, and/or reproduced on paper to be distributed to each participant.] Inform the class that this is how the chapter on mission in the *Book of Order* begins. Suggest that this sentence summarizes the contents of the chapter. As four notes announce what Beethoven's Fifth Symphony is about, this sentence prepares us for what we are to find out about mission.

F. Inquire how the group reacts to this definition. It is admittedly general or abstract. The various reactions will help you understand more fully the various views represented. Indicate that these reactions will be noted, and revisited at the end of the study.

G. Identify the key words in G-3.0100, which are as follows:

    1. Church

    2. God

    3. World

    4. Bible

    5. Faith

    6. Form

Use the discussion in the Introduction to help the participants begin to understand that these are the basic themes or
"notes" on which the mission symphony is based. As an
exercise, the participants might be divided into groups with
highlighters to count the number of times each of the key
words appears, as well as where. As the groups report, ask
whether they found anything interesting about where these
terms were grouped.

H. Indicate the schedule of meetings for this study, and request
that the participants read chapter 1 for the next meeting.

II. God's Activity and Mission

A. As participants arrive:

1. Select some march music in 4/4 time, such as the old
hymn from *The Hymnbook* "God Is Working His Purpose
Out" or "Arise, Your Light Has Come (Hymn 411), or
Psalm 104 sung as "Bless the Lord, My Soul and Being."
An alternative would be to have some stirring march, perhaps by John Philip Sousa, played by a band playing in the
background.

2. Display a flowchart highlighting the key events of God's
activity recited in G-3.0100.

3. Display the phrase from G-3.0100 so that all may see
it: "The mission of the Church is given form by God's
activity. . . . "

B. Begin by asking the group how they feel when they hear a
march. Many of us find energy from marches, which we
sometimes call "stirring."

1. Comment that the music which was playing as the class
began was a march. Point to the opening statement of
G-3.0100, that God's activity gives form to the Church's
mission, beginning in the Old Testament.

2. Have the group identify the seven active verbs in G-3.0101.
a. G-3.0101a: "created, made, did not forsake, chose"
b. G-3.0100b: "liberated, covenanted, confronted"

3. Other verbs indicating God's activity in these two
paragraphs are:
a. G-3.0101a: "charging, responding"
b. G-3.0100b: "judging, sustaining"

4. Discuss this thumbnail portrait of God's activity in the Old Testament with such questions as these:
   a. What surprises do you find in this depiction?
   b. Does this portrait offer a reasonably biblical understanding of God at work in the Old Testament?
   c. How well does this portrait convey the sense of an active God?

C. Note that the shift from G-3.0101 to G-3.0102 indicates the major change from Old to New Testament.
   1. Jesus Christ is born, God-incarnate.
   2. God acts through Jesus Christ
     a. Announces good news to the poor
     b. Proclaims release to the captives
     c. Recovers sight for the blind
     d. Frees broken victims
     e. Proclaims the year of God's favor
   3. Have the participants identify connections as well as differences between G-3.0100 and G-3.0102. Keep the conversation connected to the text, which will highlight the specific intention of the passage.

D. Point out that G-3.0103 introduces the Holy Spirit, and the tempo changes to 3/4, a waltz.
   1. Inquire of the group, Where does one hear 3/4 music, except in church?
   2. Suggest that the group identify why the tone of this paragraph differs from the previous two.
   3. Invite participants to identify two-word phrases, as a way of uncovering how this paragraph differs from the previous ones. These phrases are:
     a. "redeeming and reconciling"
     b. "presence and power"
     c. "individuals and societies"
     d. "repentance and obedience"

E. Conclude the session by having the group ponder two questions:
   1. What themes do they find that flow through G-3.0100?
   2. What implications for Christian life and mission do they find in this section?
   3. Remind the group of the assignment for next week: Chapter 2 of *Mission Symphony*.

III. Church and Mission

Note: Your preparation for this session should include a careful review of *Book of Confessions* 6.140–.145, Westminster Confession, Chapter 25. "Church" when capitalized in the *Book of Order,* and especially in this section, refers to the visible Church *Book of Confessions* (6.141), not the Presbyterian Church (U.S.A.). The remaining three paragraphs deal with some implications of this reference. Your degree of clarity on this point will assist the group in grasping this part of the study.

A. As participants arrive:

1. Set the tone for this session by playing a CD of a fugue by Johann Sebastian Bach, ideally something from his "English Suite." This work is fairly complex, yet is also melodic. Some groups might find the jazz metaphor more accessible, where different musicians playing an instrument they understand work together to bring out new depth to a specific tune.

2. Display a dictionary definition of fugue as a type of music for those who may be unfamiliar with the term. (The word has another, less pleasant meaning.)

B. Discuss the fugue form of music. Some may find it confusing or weird. Emphasize the interweaving of various themes, which interact so that the result is a richness beyond a single line of melody.

C. Display so all can read (or provide handouts) with the text of the following:

G-3.0200, "The Church of Jesus Christ . . . "

G-3.0200a, "The Church is called to be a sign"

G-3.0300c, "The Church is called to be . . . evangelist"

1. Initiate a comparison of the two statements, asking such questions as

a. Which of the three "definitions" initially appeals to you more than the other?

b. Explain what attracts you to one of these definitions.

c. Identify the word or words you don't understand.

d. Discuss the meaning of the word *Church* in these definitions. Why is it capitalized? How does "Presbyterian Church (U.S.A.) relate to this word?

2. Focus on the phrase in G-3.0200a, " . . . called to be a sign in and for the world. . . . "

      a. Who makes the call? How does this connect with what God has already done?

      b. How can the church be a "sign"?

   3. What does "the new reality" mean in G-3.0200b? What more familiar terms are included? How does this expression affect you?

   4. Discuss how adequately the three subheads in G-3.0200b (1), (2), (3) summarize and extend God's activity as described in the G-3.0100–.0200).

      a. Consider how these three mission foci may be considered a fugue, with each theme contributing to the faithfulness to God's intent as shown in the material studied in the previous session.

      b. Assist the group in appreciating how "diversity of gifts" helps understand those who emphasize one or the other of these three mission foci as predominant.

  D. Delve into the implications of G-3.0200c by considering the importance of:

   1. Personal and corporate dimensions of being the body of Christ.

   2. Mission as giving "shape and substance" to the truth of Paul's metaphor of the body of Christ.

  E. Conclude with a summary of the progress to date, and highlighting the topic and assignment for the next session.

IV. The Church's Calling to Mission

  A. As participants arrive:

   1. Set the mood for the session with a CD of Johann Sebastian Bach's "English Suite," or some other baroque counterpoint. The reason is to offer an example of how multiple lines of music can become moving and pleasant.

   2. Display the following items, so that participants may browse as they gather:

      a. The map "Our Mission Workers around the World" from the *Presbyterian Planning Calendar.*

      b. At least one copy of the *Mission Yearbook* for the current year. The center section might be removed as a separate piece. The pages for your synod and presbytery might also be separated for the information of the group.

    c. The three mission agencies report annually to the General Assembly. Their reports are included in the *Minutes of the General Assembly,* which your pastor receives in the early fall. Other articles or books related to mission, including material gleaned from www.pcusa.org/mission. Other resources are suggested at the end of this guide.

B. Distribute copies of the words to "When I Had Not Yet Learned of Jesus," no. 410 in the *Presbyterian Hymnal.* Decide how many verses to use.

    1. Have the group read the words together. If there are singers in the group, they might lead in the singing of this hymn from Korea.

    2. Read the parable of the talents, Matthew 25:14–30. Comment that the *Software edition* of *The Presbyterian Hymnal* suggests that this hymn written in 1967 was a reflection by a Korean Presbyterian on this parable.

    3. Discuss whether the hymn summarizes what we have studied thus far.

C. Point out that the text of G-3.0300 uses *call* three times, as the major verb governing three distinct emphases of this material. This may be done various ways. The following are two suggestions.

Suggestion A

    1. Divide the group into three, assigning each group to summarize what the assigned call might mean for the Church in general, and your church in particular. Indicate that they have ten minutes for this assignment, and then each group will share their understanding with the total group.

    2. Circulate among the groups, listening to their conversation, responding to their questions, providing encouragement.

    3. Have each group report to the others their understanding and/or learning to the whole group.

    4. Conclude the session by a celebration of the diversity of calls for the diversity of gifts in our denomination.

Suggestion B

    1. Have resources regarding the mission program of the Presbyterian Church (U.S.A) open and distributed around the room. Invite the people to browse through these, seeking one that they find particularly interesting.

2. Divide the group into threes, to share what they have found with one another for five minutes.

3. Ask each group to identify which of the "calls" in G-3.0300 is related to each of the mission activities they selected. Suggest that an activity may be a response to more than one call.

4. Conclude the session by a celebration of the diversity of calls for the diversity of gifts in our denomination.

V. Mission and Risk

A. As participants arrive:

In addition to the music suggested at the beginning of chapter 4, you might choose one or two hymns from the index headings "Irregular" and "Irregular with Refrain" on page 705 of *The Presbyterian Hymnal*. The software edition comes with electronic sound, which might be played for the group if they are timid in trying new material. Appendix 1 presents the titles, numbers, and sources of these thirty-eight hymns. Note also that many of these come as a result of mission work of various sorts.

B. Have the participants sing one or two of the "irregular" hymns.

1. Discuss the group's attitude toward the music.

2. Explore with the group how the music related to the text of each hymn.

3. Distribute copies of Appendix 1, then discuss what this suggests about the fruits of mission.

C. Distribute copies, or have the group find in their copies of the book, G-3.0400.

1. Read the passage over together in unison.

2. Invite the participants to share their initial reaction to this material.

3. Remind the class that the risk of the Church is consistent with our understanding of Jesus' resurrection.

4. Have the group consider how the Church's mission is a risky enterprise.

D. Introduce the notion of God's call to the group.

1. Read a passage such as Isaiah 6 for an instance of how God calls.

2. Divide the people into four groups, and assign each group one of the subheadings (a, b, c, d) of G-3.0401.

    a. Have each group read their assignment and consider it together.

    b. Invite each group to draw one implication from their assigned call for your church.

    c. Gather all groups together, and hear from each group.

E. Summarize the session, then ask the group to ponder what they have learned, and be prepared to suggest implications for your church.

VI. What Are We Going to Do?

A. As participants arrive:
Display again the resources you gathered for the class. Set the mood by laying again some of the music which the group appreciated in earlier sessions.

B. Invite each person to share something they discovered during the sessions. Establish the ground rule that discussion and comment will follow when every person has made their contribution.

C. Propose a brainstorming session regarding what the group would suggest the church do in responding to what the group has learned.

    1. List the proposed actions so all can see.

    2. Discuss which of these the group considers most urgent.

    3. Develop a plan for putting the proposal(s) into action.

    4. Identify those willing to assist with the project.

    or

D. Have the group turn to the Directory for Worship, chapters 6 and 7 (W-6.0000, 7.0000).

    1. Assign small groups to look at sections of this material, and determine how they are (or are not) related to G-3.0000 for ten minutes or so.

    2. Invite each group to report their findings, as well as any discoveries they make.

    3. Consider what this means for the group, and for the church.

E. Close with a circle prayer seeking guidance and strength to respond to Christ's call to mission.

ADDITIONAL RESOURCES

Books

From the series *The Presbyterian Presence: The Twentieth Century Experience* (Louisville: Westminster Press), by title of article and volume:

Grayson L. Tucker, "Enhancing Church Vitality through Congregational Change," in *The Mainstream Protestant "Decline"* (1990), pp. 68–74, deals with how mission relates to the vitality of a church.

The index of *The Organizational Revolution: Presbyterians and American Denominationalism* (1992) has numerous references to "mission(s)" in its index (p. 385), offering a rich combination of historical data regarding mission in our denomination.

John R. Fitzmier and Randall Balmer, "A Poultice for the Bite of the Cobra: The Hocking Report and Presbyterian Missions in the Middle Decade of the Twentieth Century" in *The Diversity of Discipleship: The Presbyterians and Twentieth-Century Christian Witness* (1991), pp. 105–125, deals with the foreign mission history of Presbyterians from 1930 to 1970.

James H. Smylie, *A Brief History of the Presbyterians* (Louisville: Geneva Press, 1996), offers a historical portrait of mission as a part of the Presbyterian story. The index of subjects on page 159 lists the specific references to mission.

Other Media

Each year there is a *Mission Yearbook for Prayer and Study* that provides one-page descriptions of presbytery, synod, and General

Assembly mission emphases. The alphabetical listing in the front enables one to find the discussion of work by agency and geographic area. *The Mission Yearbook* available from Presbyterian Distribution Service. Call (800) 524-2612 and ask for PDS 70-612-04-450.

Nancy Hamilton has prepared the "General Assembly Council Mission Policy Guide: A Directory of Current Mission Policies, Position Statements, Strategies, Guidelines, and Actions of the Presbyterian Church (U.S.A.)," 115 pages. Copies can be obtained by calling Alejandra Sherman, (888) 788-7228, ext. 5580.

The Worldwide Ministries Division publishes *WMD Highlights* twice a year. This is a sixteen-page magazine of stories about people and projects. To obtain copies, contact Presbyterian Distribution Service, (800) 524-2612, ask for PDS 74-280-03-008, and indicate the number of free copies you need.

The 215th General Assembly (2003) approved "Gathering for God's Future: A Renewed Call to Worldwide Mission." This is available at www.pcusa.org, clicking on "U.S. and World Mission," then clicking on Worldwide Ministries.

There are two accessible collections of mission stories by former Moderator Marge Carpenter: *To the Ends of the Earth* (1995); *And a Little Bit Farther* (1998), both available from Geneva Press. Using a story from one of these to open each class session would heighten the interest of the class.

Numerous other reports and materials are available for inspection and order at the other options on the "U.S. and World Mission" page. If possible, a session exploring these pages might be interesting and helpful for the group.

Your presbytery resource center will have other resources for your use.